Starting with the Bible

STEPHEN TRAVIS

STARTING WITH THE BIBLE

A LION BOOK

Published by
Lion Publishing plc
Sandy Lane West, Oxford, England
ISBN 0 7459 4160 5

First edition 1994
This combined edition 1999
10 9 8 7 6 5 4 3 2 1 0

A catalogue record for this book is available
from the British Library

Printed and bound in Malaysia

Contents

Starting with the
Old Testament

1

What's in the Old Testament for us?

● ● ● ● ● ● ● ● ● ● ● ● ●

'I never knew such a God existed.' The speaker taught chemistry in an Indian university. He had grown up in one of India's oppressed groups, despised and exploited by higher social classes. Determined to get his own back on those who oppressed him and his community, he threw himself into his education and went to college committed to the revolutionary ideals of Marxism.

At college he was given a Bible by some Christian students and read it out of casual interest. There in the Old Testament he discovered a God who constantly takes the side of the poor against their oppressors; a God who cared enough about the everyday lives of ordinary people to make laws about their safety, laws to protect them against being bullied by the rich and powerful; a God who is just and expects justice among the people he has created.

'I never knew such a God existed,' he said. But he also read—still in the Old Testament—of a God who forgives, a God 'slow to anger and abounding in love and faithfulness'.

He found that harder to take. 'I was attracted to the God of justice and holiness. I ran away from a God of love.' But the God of love couldn't let him go. Christian friends explained more of how God's love reaches us through Jesus Christ. And he experienced for himself the love of the God whom he had met in the pages of the Old Testament.

The Old Testament isn't just an old book full of do's and don'ts. It isn't a collection of fairy stories. Old it certainly is. But it still speaks to questions which people face today:

◆ **Why was the world made?**

◆ **Why do innocent people suffer?**

◆ **How are we meant to care for each other in society?**

◆ **Is history just a meaningless sequence of events, or is it going somewhere?**

◆ **Will God listen to my anger, my doubts, my questions as well as to my worship?**

The Old Testament isn't just a book full of do's and don'ts. It still speaks to questions which people face today.

Is the Old Testament still relevant today?

People often assume that because the Old Testament is old it no longer has value. An old painting may be worth millions. A truth discovered long ago—for example, the truth that the earth goes round the sun—is as true today as when it was first discovered. But an old book, we tend to think, belongs to a bygone age. It cannot speak to a world of nuclear power and genetic engineering.

And Christians who value the New Testament are inclined to dismiss the Old Testament as inferior and no longer necessary. After all, it was Christians who took the Hebrew scriptures and called them the 'Old Testament', implying that they now had something better.

Can the Old Testament be relevant in a world of nuclear power and genetic engineering?

But there are strong reasons why the Old Testament should not be dismissed so easily.

◆ **Though the Old Testament doesn't deal with many of the specific issues of modern life, the really important things about human nature remain the same now as then.**

The Old Testament deals with the great issues of our experience—the contradictions between good and evil within us, the use and abuse of power, our longing for security and for a better world, our grappling with doubt and suffering, our search for shape and purpose in our lives.

◆ **To ignore it is to undervalue the great contribution of the Jewish people to human wisdom and our understanding of God.**

The legal systems of much of the world depend on the foundation of the Ten Commandments, and the Old Testament images of God, for example as the good shepherd, have spread far beyond their original settings in Palestine.

10

◆ **From a Christian viewpoint, the Old Testament belongs with the New, as the two acts of a two-act play belong together.**

Much of the important action occurs in Act Two. But if you don't see Act One you can't understand how the events of Act Two are significant. The Old Testament tells a story which points forward to the coming of the Messiah; the New Testament tells how the Messiah came and what he can mean for the whole world. And Jesus himself showed a thorough knowledge of the Old Testament.

◆ **The New Testament doesn't ignore the Old Testament but builds on it.**

It assumes the Old Testament's understanding of God, of care for the created world, of sexual love and of human creativity in art and music. It sees no need to repeat the deep insights of the Hebrew Scriptures into human suffering or the need for justice in society. On these and many other issues the Old Testament has more to say than the New.

◆ **As a matter of experience, people today continue to find that God speaks to them through the Old Testament writings.**

They are challenged and guided by its moral and social demands. They speak and listen to God through the Psalms. They see the patterns of God's work in their own lives as they read how he acted in Israel's history. Reading and hearing his book, they are drawn closer to him.

Reading and hearing the Old Testament, people are drawn closer to God.

2

Finding your way around

● ● ● ● ● ● ● ● ● ● ● ● ●

'I don't often visit our local library. To be honest, I'm embarrassed about not knowing where to find things.

'Everyone else seems to know exactly where to look for the romantic novels they want, or the books on sport or gardening. I know there are assistants there to help, but won't they think I'm silly for not understanding their ways of arranging things?'

Many people feel like that about the Old Testament.

It's too large, too full of ancient books with no clues about how to get started on them. And if you begin at the beginning it's OK for a while. But then you get stuck in complex rules about things like what to do with a dangerous bull and how to run a harvest festival.

Thankfully, every Bible has a contents page, so that if you're looking for the book of Joshua or Proverbs you can easily find out where it begins. And many modern

The books of the Old Testament

The Old Testament isn't just one book - it's thirty-nine of them. Some parts of the Christian Church - Roman Catholics, for example - include a number of other books in their Bibles. These are known as Deutero-canonical books.

THE LAW

Genesis
Exodus
Leviticus
Numbers
Deuteronomy

HISTORY AND STORY

Joshua
Judges
Ruth
1 Samuel
2 Samuel
1 Kings
2 Kings
1 Chronicles
2 Chronicles
Ezra
Nehemiah
Esther

POETRY AND WISDOM

Job
Psalms
Proverbs
Ecclesiastes
Song of Solomon

PROPHETS

Isaiah
Jeremiah
Lamentations
Ezekiel
Daniel
Hosea
Joel
Amos
Obadiah
Jonah
Micah
Nahum
Habakkuk
Zephaniah
Haggai
Zechariah
Malachi

Bibles have a short introduction to each biblical book to give you clues about how to approach it. You will find this, for example, in some editions of the *Good News Bible* and of the *New International Version*.

The Old Testament is actually a collection of thirty-nine books written over hundreds of years. The Jews divided it into three parts:

◆ **The Law (or 'Pentateuch') was the first five books.**

◆ **The Prophets included not only the books of prophets like Isaiah (which they called 'the latter prophets') but also the historical books from Joshua to 2 Chronicles ('the former prophets'). The reason for this was that the Jews saw 'history' not simply as a record of events but as the arena in which God acts and speaks. Both 'former' and 'latter' prophets were accounts of how God acted and spoke to his people Israel.**

◆ **The Writings were all the other books— including the poetry of Psalms and Job, short stories like Ruth and Esther, and the love poem called the Song of Songs.**

When the Hebrew Bible was translated into Greek for the benefit of Jews and others who were not very familiar with Hebrew, the order of the books was changed. There were now four sections—the Law, History and Story, Poetry and Wisdom books, and Prophets. This is the arrangement followed in most English Bibles.

In addition, more divisions were added later: into chapter and verse. This makes it easier to find a specific part of a particular book of the Old Testament. For instance, there are two books of Samuel. So the reference 1 Samuel 3:2 will mean the first book of Samuel, chapter 3, verse 2.

The first book of
Samuel
   chapter 3
      verse 2

1 Samuel 3 : 2

> *I found consolation in the Bible. Not 'This is just a test' kind of consolation, but comfort from the real, immediate voices of people who had suffered greatly, and in ways that seemed close to what I was going through. I read the Bible more than fifty times in those first few years.*
>
> Terry Anderson, hostage in Lebanon
> (to journalists on his release)

When you read a modern book, it helps to know at the start what kind of a book it is. We have different expectations, and different ways of reading, a detective novel, a biography or a cookery book. When we read the Old Testament, it helps to know what kind of a book it is that we are reading. We will approach Psalms in a different way from Joshua, for example—one is poetry, the other is history.

There is a whole library here, reflecting the variety of people's experiences of God and responses to him. It can speak to our many different needs and situations. It's not always easy to get into, but it's worth the effort!

A created world

The book of Genesis begins with an account of the creation of the world: 'In the beginning God created the heavens and the earth' (Genesis 1:1). The God who wants to make himself known to men and women is responsible for the whole of creation.

The story in Genesis 1 isn't a scientific report about how the world began. Science has its own contribution to make to our understanding of the origins of the world. But the Bible has something to say through this story which science cannot say: not *how* the world was made, but *why*. The world didn't happen by chance, but is the product of a purposeful Creator.

Human beings tend to be most interested in their own place in God's creation. But most of Genesis 1 focuses on the rest of the created world—sun, moon, plants and animals, and so on. Humanity is the climax of God's creative plan, but not the be-all and end-all.

This is a vital message for today's world. The instruction that we should 'rule over' the rest of creation doesn't give us permission to exploit it. We abuse our responsibility if we turn forests into deserts, put animal species out of existence or pollute the atmosphere with the results of our extravagant use of natural resources.

For 'ruling' is the role of a king or queen. And in the Bible, monarchs are expected to use their power as God uses power—with care for those committed to their charge.

To be human involves sharing in God's care for the world—both the whole human race and the natural world—because we are entrusted with that responsibility by God himself.

The story of God and his people

● ● ● ● ● ● ● ● ● ● ● ● ● ●

The Old Testament is full of stories. But they are all part of one big story. It is the story of God inviting a particular group of people to get to know him, so that in the long run the whole world may learn to know and love him.

Before looking at the different parts of the Old Testament it will help us to have a sense of the overall story of what happened to those people. It goes something like this...

A long time ago there was a man called Abraham who lived in the land between the Euphrates and Tigris rivers, in modern Iraq. God told him to move with his family to Canaan, four hundred miles away. God promised to provide a homeland there for his descendants, and to make of them a special nation through whom the whole world would find blessing.

Abraham's family prospered in Canaan for three generations. But a famine caused them to seek refuge in Egypt. There after a while they became slaves, working on the building projects of the Egyptian kings, the pharaohs.

The Land

Today's debates over possession of the land of Israel echo a central theme of the Old Testament.

At the beginning of the history of the Jewish people, Abraham received from God the promise: 'To your offspring I will give this land' (Genesis 12:7). It was to be a place of security, a place which they could call home and where their special relationship with God could develop.

They conquered it under Joshua, defended it under the kings, and lost it to the Assyrians and Babylonians. On their return from exile in Babylon they lived in it, but always under the rule of a foreign power—except for the years 142–63BC.

It is striking that the land is constantly referred to in the Old Testament as 'the land of the Canaanites'. They never forgot that it had belonged to another race. And Old Testament writers speak of it as God's gift, not as Israel's right.

If God had given it to them, he could also withdraw his protection when they turned away from him. The exile wasn't merely a national tragedy, it was an act of divine judgment on Israel's failure to live by God's law.

God gave to the people of Israel 'the most beautiful of all lands' (Ezekiel 20:6). But an Israel which fails to show justice and compassion to the vulnerable 'will not remain in the Lord's land' (Hosea 9:3). God's gifts can never be taken for granted.

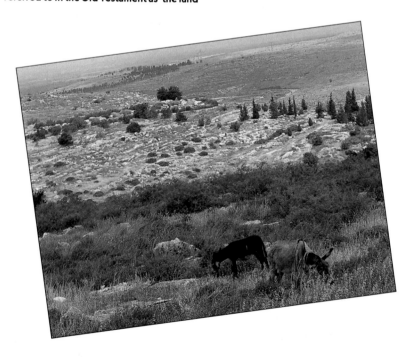

But God hadn't forgotten them. He told a man called Moses to lead the people—now called Israelites—in a dramatic escape out of Egypt. This 'exodus' involved the miraculous crossing of the 'Red Sea'. The water was held back while the Israelites crossed over, and then poured down on Egyptian soldiers to prevent their pursuit of the escaping slaves.

During forty years of wandering through the desert to get back to Canaan, God gave them the Law which became the basis of their life as a people. And they always looked back to the exodus as God's very special act of liberation. They knew him as the God who acts in history to deliver the oppressed.

Under Joshua, Moses' successor, they established themselves in Canaan, 'the Promised Land'. But they constantly felt the threat of attack by neighbouring nations.

They wanted a king to make them more secure, and God gave them Saul, then David and Solomon. David especially was a great king who made their land secure against its enemies. Later generations saw David's reign as a golden age, an ideal time which they longed for God to repeat. Solomon was important as the builder of the temple, the centre of Israelite worship in Jerusalem.

But the danger of kings is that they come to enjoy their power too much. Solomon's son Rehoboam was oppressive, and most of the nation rebelled against him. They formed the northern kingdom of Israel, whilst Rehoboam and his successors retained the southern area around Jerusalem, known as Judah.

The northern kingdom lasted for two hundred years as a separate state, until it fell to the aggressive Assyrians. Many of its people were taken into exile in other parts of Assyria's empire, never again to return to their own land.

Judah continued for a further 135 years before another empire brought the kingdom to its end. Nebuchadnezzar of Babylon ravaged the land, destroyed

The Israelites always looked back to the exodus—their escape from slavery in Egypt—as God's act of liberation.

The story of Abraham and his descendants

1 (AROUND 1900 BC) Abraham leaves the city of Ur in Mesopotamia and journeys to the land of Canaan. He spends some time in Egypt in order to avoid a famine, and then returns to Canaan. He lives a nomadic lifestyle, and as he travels throughout Canaan, God promises him that all the land he sees will one day belong to his descendants.

2 (BETWEEN 1650 AND 1270 BC) Abraham's grandson Jacob and his children settle in Egypt. As their numbers increase they are seen as a threat by the rulers of Egypt who force them into slave labour.

Moses confronts the Egyptian pharaoh and leads the Israelites out of Egypt and into the desert. At Mount Sinai God gives them his laws. He instructs them to invade Canaan, but those sent to spy out the land return with a discouraging report. They remain in the desert 40 years before attacking Jericho and beginning the conquest of the land.

3 (1230 BC) The Israelites settle the land promised to Abraham and become the nation of Israel. But political tensions divide the country (930 BC) into the northern kingdom of Israel, with its capital at Samaria, and southern Judah with its capital at Jerusalem.

20

4 (722–538 BC) Israel generally rejects God, and the country is overrun by the Assyrians (green arrow), who take the people captive and scatter them throughout their huge empire.

The people of Judah vacillate between serving God and ignoring him. Judah survives Assyrian attacks, but later falls to Nebuchadnezzar, king of Babylon (blue arrow). The people of Judah are taken as prisoners to Babylon (red arrow). They remain there for 70 years until the Persians sack the city (brown arrow) and allow the Jews to return to Jerusalem.

The map indicates present-day boundaries: Persia is modern Iran.

Through much of history, the kingdoms of Israel and Judah were occupied by foreign powers—from the Assyrians and Babylonians to the Romans.

Jerusalem, and took all its leading citizens into exile in Babylon.

It was a devastating blow for a nation who believed that they enjoyed God's special protection. What price now their status as God's special people? Why had God let it happen?

Throughout the period of the kingdoms of Israel and Judah, God sent prophets, people who would communicate his will and explain his intentions to the people. Frequently they warned that the people's troubles were due to their ignoring God's will. They spoke of the consequences of disobedience, and the blessings which would come to an obedient people. But for most of the time the rulers and the people took no notice.

So disaster struck. But still God didn't forget them. In Babylon the Jews were able to maintain their religious and community life. And after fifty years Babylon itself fell victim to King Cyrus of Persia. He allowed Jewish people to return to their land and rebuild their lives.

Despite economic and social problems the temple was in due course rebuilt. Under Nehemiah the walls of Jerusalem were restored. Under Ezra the Law was written down and was listened to with new seriousness.

But still the Jews lived under Persian rule. They longed for freedom. Prophets spoke of a coming king who would set them free from all their enemies. But Persian rule gave way to rule by Alexander the Great of Greece, and then by Syrians.

The Syrian ruler Antiochus tried to force Jews to give up their faith. A loyal Jew named Judas, together with his brothers, led the 'Maccabean Revolt' against Antiochus. Their guerrilla tactics were successful, and for eighty years the Jews enjoyed independence from foreign control. Then came the Romans, who allowed the half-Jew Herod the Great to rule the land. Not until 1948 would there again be an independent Jewish state.

Christianity is inexplicable without Judaism. It simply is not possible to understand the world of the New Testament in isolation from its roots in the Near East and particularly against the background of Jewish culture, theology and life.

George Carey, Archbishop of Canterbury

The Jews believed that God acted in their history. They believed that God had given them the Law to show how they were meant to live as his people. But time and again they found themselves asking, 'How long, O Lord? How long till we are free from oppression? How long till we know in full the blessing you promised to Abraham?'

Yet through all that waiting they were discovering more of God, so that they could reveal God to the nations of the world. The Old Testament is their story. And it is God's story, recording how he made himself known during hundreds of years of history.

4

Laying the foundations

● ● ● ● ● ● ● ● ● ● ● ● ● ●

The first five books of the Bible belong
together. The Jews called them 'the Law'. But
they are much more than a collection of rules
and regulations. The Hebrew word *Torah*
means not just 'law' but 'guidance',
'instruction'. The Law laid the foundations of
God's relationship with people.

These books offer guidance through stories
as much as through lists of do's and don'ts.
God makes himself known through events and
experiences in people's lives.

The book of **Genesis** can be divided into two parts. The
first part, chapters 1–11, sets Israel's story in the context
of the world's story. So it begins with the world's
creation. It then tells how human beings—Adam and
Eve—challenge God's will for their lives. It shows how
wrongdoing creeps into every aspect of human
relationships and destroys our relationship with God.

But in Genesis 12–50 God makes a fresh start. His
calling of Abraham and his descendants is his love in
action. They are to be a 'pilot plant', a 'prototype', of the
kind of life in relationship to him which he wants people

24

Abraham—receiver of promises

Abraham stands at the beginning of the story of God's people. To this day Jews speak of 'our father Abraham', and Christians too see him as a great example of trust in God.

His story, told in Genesis 11:27–25:11, cannot be checked historically with sources outside the Bible. Yet the social customs and the names which appear in this narrative fit with what archaeologists have discovered about conditions in the Middle East in the period 2000–1700BC.

Abraham was a city-dweller in the area which today is called Iraq. Prompted by God, he abandoned that lifestyle and set out with his family for the land of Canaan, 450 miles away. This journey was God's way of calling a person, a family, a nation to be the special bearers of his promise of blessing to the world.

When God called Abraham he promised to give him a land to live in, and descendants who would multiply to become a great nation. And he promised that through him all nations would find blessing.

Abraham's story tells of God's promise, obstacles which threatened that promise, and Abraham's faith which held on to the promise. As the story unfolds, God's promise comes under constant threat. How can Abraham and his family make their home in Canaan? It is already inhabited by Canaanites. His wife Sarah can't have children, so how can he have descendants? How can he make his home in the land when famine forces him to seek refuge in Egypt? But God's promises hold good, and so does Abraham's trust.

Even so, Abraham and Sarah are no too-good-to-be-true characters. While in Egypt Abraham saves his own skin by pretending that Sarah is his sister and making her marry the pharaoh. He goes along with her suggestion of having a child by her slave Hagar (which was a local custom). And Sarah laughs in disbelief that a woman past the menopause should have a baby.

Yet Abraham's faith shines through. He takes God at his word and does what he says. When called to leave the city for a nomadic life in Canaan, he goes. When he looks at the countless stars in the sky and senses God saying to him that his descendants will be as numerous as that, he believes him. He is always looking forward, trusting that the future is in God's hand, and sure enough, he and Sarah do have a son, Isaac.

But what can we make of that strange and troubling story in which God 'tested Abraham' by telling him to kill Isaac as a sacrifice? For Abraham the problem wasn't only that the idea seemed barbaric. To kill his son would be to destroy the one through whom God's promise of descendants was to be fulfilled.

The writer tells us that God's purpose was to test Abraham, to strengthen his faith. Abraham didn't know that. But though he must have been full of anguish at the danger to his son, he obeyed. His faith involved being willing to give up what was most dear to him. And he obeyed even when he couldn't see how God's plan would work out.

Sometimes people believe that God is calling them to act in a certain way, but can't see the purpose in it. Like Abraham, we can't see the end from the beginning. His story challenges us to risk everything for the sake of obedience to God. And it encourages us to trust that God's purpose will make sense in the long run.

Genesis 12–20

God calls Abraham
12:1–3

A child for Sarah
17:15–22, 21:1–7

The sacrifice of Isaac
22:1–19

Jacob tricks his brother
27:1–41

Joseph's story
37, 39–47

The covenant or agreement between God and the people of Israel is at the heart of the book of Exodus

of all races eventually to experience.

Here then are stories full of drama and suspense. Will Abraham's wife Sarah have a baby, even though she is past the usual child-bearing age? Yes, because God will not fail to keep his promise to Abraham and Sarah that their descendents will become a great people.

There are stories about Abraham's son Isaac, and about Jacob, Isaac's scoundrel son. And then there is the story of Jacob's favourite son Joseph, a young man whose dreams fuelled big ideas about himself. He was sold as a slave by his jealous brothers and taken by traders to Egypt. There his skill at interpreting dreams eventually brought him to the pharaoh's attention and he was made Minister of Food Storage and Distribution—the second most powerful man in the kingdom.

Famine in Canaan forced Jacob's family to seek help in Egypt and brought them face to face with Joseph. In the end he and his brothers were reconciled and they all enjoyed the benefits of Joseph's wise planning.

The book of **Exodus** focuses on the role of Moses as Israel's liberator and lawgiver. After the famine Joseph's relations had settled in Egypt. But as they grew and prospered they became targets for the tyranny of later pharaohs. Moses, who had had a profound experience of God in the desert, was God's man for this moment.

The heart of the book is in chapters 19–20. In chapter 20 God gives the people the Ten Commandments. But before that, in chapter 19, he reminds them of what he has already done by rescuing them from Egypt and speaks of the 'covenant' or 'agreement' which he is making with them.

In other words, God first acts to rescue people and bring them into relationship with himself. Then he gives them laws—guidance to keep the relationship healthy. In the Old Testament as in the New, God in his love makes the first move towards humanity, and calls us to respond in obedience.

Moses—liberator and lawgiver

As a Hebrew child brought up in an Egyptian palace, we might expect Moses to opt for a life of peace and luxury. But no. He became the leader of his enslaved people and challenged the tyranny of the Egyptian empire. God's message to the pharoah, 'Let my people go,' became his slogan. And in the end the pharaoh had no choice. He was helpless to stop Moses leading the Israelites from slavery to the Promised Land.

Such leadership didn't come easily to Moses. Like many of the Bible's great leaders, he was a reluctant hero. 'Who am I? How can I do it?' were his questions when he sensed God's call to lead the Israelites out of Egypt. 'I'll be with you,' said God. 'That's all the reassurance you need.'

So Moses argued with the pharaoh. He warned the pharaoh of the plagues which would afflict Egypt if he didn't show mercy to the Israelites. The pharaoh didn't change his mind, and the plagues came. Most of them were probably a series of natural phenomena following an unusually high flooding of the Nile—God using the workings of nature for his own purpose.

Finally, in the aftermath of the most terrible plague—the death of each first-born Egyptian son—the Israelites left Egypt. The pharaoh still tried to get his slave labour back by sending the army after them, only to have all the Egyptian soldiers and their chariots overwhelmed by the Red Sea which the Israelites had just crossed as though it were dry land.

The key event on the long journey to Canaan, the land promised to Abraham, whose descendents they were, took place at Mount Sinai. There God extended the 'covenant' agreement which he had already made with Abraham, by which he was committed to his people and they to him. In particular, he spelt out how they should respond to him by giving them the Ten Commandments.

There are many other laws in the books from Exodus to Deuteronomy, all of which Jews came to associate with Moses. They are, in a sense, an expansion of the basic commandments given at Sinai. Many of them remain today a challenge to the way we treat other people, such as: 'Do not ill-treat an alien or oppress him, for you were aliens in Egypt' and 'If you see the donkey of someone who hates you fallen down under its load, do not leave it there; be sure you help him with it'.

The people in the Bible are really alive. The things that bothered them, the temptations they were subject to, are just as relevant today.

I empathize with Moses because he came from two cultures; he was an Israelite brought up in Egypt. I come from two cultures: Jamaican and English. He was a very shy person and I'm very shy. I can understand how frightened he must have been of the things God asked him to do.

God still speaks through the Bible. It's a very lively book!

Josephine Campbell, publisher

The book of **Leviticus** consists of instructions about worship and festivals, and about what is involved in living as a 'holy people', a nation dedicated to God.

Numbers gets its name from the census of Israelites described in chapter one. Its Hebrew name, 'In the wilderness', describes its contents better. It tells of the Israelites' journey towards the Promised Land, how God provided for their needs and how they grumbled when things got tough. The journey of faith is a hard journey. But there are lessons to be learnt on the way, and God travels with us.

The book of **Deuteronomy** (meaning 'repetition of the law') presents Moses addressing the people on the edge of the Promised Land. He reminds them of what God has done for them, how he cares for them, and what kind of response he expects of them.

The God of Deuteronomy is the Lord of history who has brought Israel from Egypt to the Promised Land. He has made Israel his special people, his 'treasured possession'. Two words describing their response to him are particularly stressed in this book: they are to *remember* what he has done, and to *love* him. This remembering and love is expressed both in worship and in sensitive obedience to his will.

Moses sets before the people two choices for their national and community life:

> *See, I set before you today life and prosperity, death and destruction. For I command you today to love the Lord your God, to walk in his ways . . . then you will live and increase, and the Lord your God will bless you in the land you are entering to possess. But if your heart turns away and you are not obedient . . . you will not live long in the land you are crossing the Jordan to enter and possess.*
>
> DEUTERONOMY 30:15–18

In the book of Deuteronomy, Moses reminds the people of Israel how God has helped them in the past, and seeks their love for the future.

28

The Ten Commandments

The nature of these commandments is often misunderstood. People think of them as a negative list of 'Thou shalt nots'. But the Ten Commandments are rules to safeguard life, not to take the joy out of it.

God is providing boundaries within which people are to live. Within those boundaries there is freedom, not imprisonment, because these laws protect society from behaviour which would destroy it. If you send a group of children into a playground and tell them they can do anything they like, the result will not be freedom but chaos, and adults are not that different.

The Commandments begin with guidance about loyalty to the one God, who has freed his people from slavery. Then they move onto social relationships. The sabbath commandment protects the rights and health of workers.

Family life is safeguarded by the requirement to honour parents and to avoid adultery. The commandment not to kill asserts the value that God sets on every human being, and justice between people demands the prohibitions on theft, false accusation and the desire for others' goods which leads to conflict.

You shall have no other gods before me

~

You shall not make for yourself an idol

~

You shall not misuse the name of the LORD your God

~

Remember the Sabbath day by keeping it holy

~

Honour your father and your mother

~

You shall not murder

~

You shall not commit adultery

~

You shall not steal

~

You shall not give false testimony

~

You shall not covet your neighbour's goods

5

God in history

●●●●●●●●●●●●●●●

If someone invited us to tell our life story we could tell it in many different ways. For example, we could focus attention on our schooldays or our sporting achievements or our family life. We could explain why we made certain decisions which altered the course of our life.

But however we told the story, we would be choosing what we felt was important to us. And we would be telling the story from a particular point of view. My version of how I came to be punished at school for 'cheating' in an exam is not the same as my teacher's version.

In the same way, the story of a nation is told by choosing certain events as being especially significant. And it is told from a particular point of view, in order to make certain points. A British army general would not tell the story of British rule of India in the same way as an Indian cotton-picker.

Writing history involves giving shape to the story.

And you give shape to it by *choosing* what you see as important and explaining *why* you think it is important.

As we have seen, the Israelites who told the story of their escape from Egypt saw it as a great act of God. He had liberated them from slavery. That isn't how the Egyptian pharaoh's official historian would have told the story! Both the writer of Genesis and the Egyptian historian could agree that the event happened. But one of them saw in it the hand of God. The other would be working overtime to cover the cracks of a national economic and military disaster.

Hebrew historians wrote a connected record of the nation's history from their entry into the Promised Land under Joshua to the Babylonian exile six hundred years later. It is in the books of **Joshua**, **Judges**, **1 and 2 Samuel** and **1 and 2 Kings**. In it they explain events from a particular viewpoint.

They see history as the arena of God's activity. And they show how the nation's fortunes rose and fell according to whether the people and their rulers took

How you write history depends on your point of view. The Israelites saw history as the arena of God's activity.

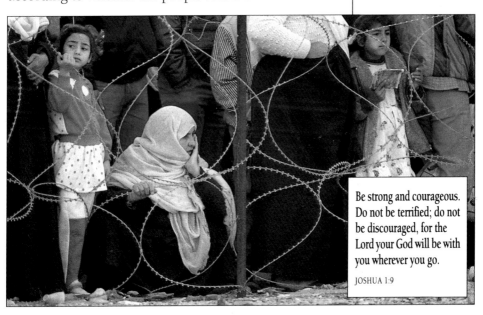

Be strong and courageous. Do not be terrified; do not be discouraged, for the Lord your God will be with you wherever you go.

JOSHUA 1:9

Ruth—from distress to hope

Tucked in between Judges and 1 Samuel, with their tales of war and politics, is the personal story of one woman, Ruth. The Israelites and the people of Moab to the east of the Jordan river were traditional enemies. But a family from Bethlehem settled in Moab during a famine. One of the men married Ruth, a Moabite woman.

After the tragic death of her husband and her father-in-law, Ruth goes with her widowed mother-in-law, Naomi, to Bethlehem, Naomi's home town. There, with Naomi's encouragement, she wins the love of another man from Naomi's family, Boaz. He marries her and brings joy to Naomi as the couple present her with a grandchild.

The story is beautifully told. But *why* is it told? In contrast to the larger-than-life characters and the national significance of the historical books, this story seems so small-scale, the people so ordinary. Perhaps that is the point, or at least part of it.

It is a story of God's involvement in the tragedies and joys of ordinary people. It shows how, at a time when violence and abuse of power hit the national headlines, there are still people living out a vivid faith in God.

Naomi, struck by the death of her husband and sons, picks up the pieces of her life and returns home. Gradually she overcomes her bitterness as she realizes that God has not abandoned her. And finally her joy is complete as she holds her grandson in her arms.

Ruth, a Moabite woman, discovers Israel's God and refuses all Naomi's pleas to do the 'sensible' thing and remain in her own country. 'Where you go I will go, and where you stay I will stay. Your people will be my people and your God my God' (Ruth 1:16). Human love can overcome the hostility of racism and nationalism.

Boaz, too, shows compassion, and acts responsibly towards his relatives and to the poor. He is an honourable man in the time of the judges—an age strewn with dishonourable men. But the dominant characters of this story are women, discovering God's care in the circumstances of ordinary life.

Two other themes are there for the reader to ponder. The fact that Ruth is not an Israelite is clearly important. The God of Israel accepts and shows faithfulness to all who come to him, whatever their background, and sometimes the people of Israel needed to be reminded of this.

And the final paragraph of the book reports that the child of Ruth and Boaz was the grandfather of King David. Israel's greatest king—and the Messiah descended from him—had a foreign woman among their ancestors!

God's law seriously. In other words, they show how God's promise and warning of Deuteronomy 30:15–18 that we looked at earlier came true in the experience of God's people.

The book of **Joshua** tells how the Israelites began to

establish themselves in Canaan. God's words to Joshua before the conquest begins are an encouragement to anyone taking on a demanding task in God's name:

Be strong and courageous. Do not be terrified; do not be discouraged, for the Lord your God will be with you wherever you go.

JOSHUA 1:9

The book of **Judges** shows how often they compromised their loyalty to God and were attacked by surrounding nations. And it records that when the people renewed their commitment to God he raised up leaders—'judges'—such as Deborah, Gideon and Samson to deliver them from their enemies.

Samuel, whose name is attached to two of these books, was a wise man of God and leader of Israel who bridged the gap between the judges and the kings. But in fact most of **1 and 2 Samuel**—the first and second books of Samuel—tell the story of the first two kings, Saul and David.

Worried about the strength of their Philistine enemies the people urged Samuel to appoint for them a king 'such as all the other nations have'. Samuel saw this as a failure of faith, a failure to trust God as their king. To want to be 'like other nations' was to deny their special calling to live by values different from those of other nations.

But God has a way of weaving even people's wrong choices into the pattern of his purpose. So he gave Israel a king—Saul. And then David, Solomon and the others who followed. The people learnt through hard experience that kings can bring not only benefits but hardships—forced labour, military conscription and taxes.

But they also learnt that God had a very special plan for David's family. One of his descendants would be the 'Messiah', God's chosen leader who would bring a new

Joshua
The fall of Jericho
5:13–6:27

Judges
Deborah
4:4–16
Gideon
6:1–8:28
Samson
13:1–16:31

1 Samuel
The people want a king
8:1–22
David and Goliath
17:12–51

2 Samuel
David and Bathsheba
11:1–12:25

David—flawed genius

David was a shepherd boy in Bethlehem when he was catapulted into the centre of his nation's history. Saul, the first king, was already proving a liability. Prompted by God, the old prophet Samuel anointed young David with oil—a sign that he was God's choice as the next king.

He soon came to Saul's attention when he killed Goliath the Philistine with a single stone from his sling. He was content to bide his time until Saul's death should open the way for David to replace him. But the popularity he gained by his feat against Goliath made Saul fiercely jealous of David. His paranoia made him try to kill David, who was forced to flee and become an outlaw.

Saul came with troops to hunt David down in his hiding place near the Dead Sea. Entering a cave to relieve himself, he had no idea that David and his friends were hiding at the back of the cave. David's friends urged him to kill Saul there and then. But he crept over and merely cut off a corner of his robe. 'I will not lift my hand against my master', he said, 'because he is the Lord's anointed'.

Saul committed suicide after losing a battle against the Philistines, and David became king first over his own tribe of Judah and then over the whole nation of Israel. He captured Jerusalem, which until then had always remained in Canaanite hands, and made it his capital city. This building of a capital in a neutral place was a shrewd move, calculated to minimize jealousy between the various tribal groups of Israel.

David squashed the power of the Philistines once and for all. He extended Israel's territory in other directions and made his country strong. He made Jerusalem the centre of Israel's worship, and received from God the promise that his son would build a temple there. Through the prophet Nathan God promised to show his love to David's descendants for ever. 'Your house and your kingdom shall endure for ever before me; your throne shall be established for ever.'

David was grateful to God for giving him success in all he did. But his next encounter with the prophet Nathan was not to be so comfortable.

One evening he looked down from the roof of his hill-top palace and saw a beautiful woman called Bathsheba bathing. A king gets used to getting what he wants, and David wanted Bathsheba. His obsession with her led him to arrange the death of her husband and to marry her.

Then Nathan came and told him a story about a rich man who stole a lamb from a poor man. David's sense of justice made him side with the poor man: 'As surely as the Lord lives, the man who did this deserves to die!'

'You're the man!', replied Nathan.

The story makes no excuses for David. He did wrong and he suffered for it. Yet he had the courage to admit his wrong and make a fresh start. So despite his mistakes he was remembered as a great king. In the books of Kings no verdict on a ruler is so positive as the words, 'He walked in all the ways of his father [ancestor] David.'

And when the Jews longed for a future king to put an end to all their troubles, it was a king 'like David' that they looked for.

kind of freedom and peace to humanity.

So Israel's desire for a king was from one viewpoint a failure of faith. Yet God made it the means through which he would show his love to humanity in a fuller way. Israel's God isn't distant and unchanging. God has given us free will to choose whether or not to obey him, but he isn't defeated by human disobedience. He adjusts to it and through it finds another way to make known his loving plan for the world.

1 and 2 Kings continue the story from Solomon's reign and his building of the temple right through to Nebuchadnezzar's destruction of Jerusalem and the exile which followed.

God rarely intervenes in dramatic or miraculous ways in these narratives. He is more like the manager of a football team than a player on the field. But all the time he is there, involved with events. All the time the nation is experiencing the truth of those words from Deuteronomy—life and blessing follow obedience to God's way, but disaster follows when people turn away from his will and his protection.

Most of 1 and 2 Kings is the story of constant compromise between trust in the living God and the old nature gods of Canaan. It is the story of a nation which has lost its vision of what it means to be God's people, showing other nations how God wants them to be.

Even the two rulers who were genuinely faithful to God—Hezekiah and Josiah—could not delay for long the judgment which was to come through the downfall of Judah and the exile to Babylon. That event in 587BC shook the faith of God's people to its foundations. But even in that disaster hope was reborn.

1 and 2 Chronicles retell the story of the books of Samuel and Kings for people of a later period. They draw out new lessons from history for Israelites returning from the Babylonian exile and trying to rebuild their lives, especially about the importance of worship.

1 Kings

The wisdom of Solomon
3:1–28

Elijah and the prophets of Baal
18:1—19:18

2 Kings

Elisha cures Naaman of leprosy
5:1–14

The siege of Jerusalem
18:13—19:36

The books of **Ezra** and **Nehemiah** continue the story from this perspective into the period after the Jews had returned from Babylon. They tell of the return to Palestine, the rebuilding of the temple, Nehemiah's rebuilding of the walls of Jerusalem and Ezra's bringing of the law back to the centre of the nation's life.

These two books grapple with the question how God's people are to relate to the world around them which does not share their faith. They show how the Persian authorities were quite sympathetic to Ezra and Nehemiah. God can use foreign powers to provide stability for his people.

2000BC	▼1800BC	▼1600BC	▼1400BC	▼1200BC
	Abraham arrives in Canaan	Abraham's descendants arrive in Egypt	Exodus from Egypt	Israelites arrive in Canaan
				D
			Moses ⬆	
	⬆ Abraham			Ruth ⬆
		Abraham's descendants living in Egypt (now known as Israelites)		Samuel ⬆
E G Y P T		The story of the Jewish people (shown by the green horizontal band) set against a background of contemporary empires.		A S S Y R I

On the other hand, the concern of the Jewish leaders to avoid the watering down of their people's unique faith led them to ban mixed marriages with non-Jews. This harsh teaching seemed necessary to them if Judaism was to maintain its distinctive mission to the world.

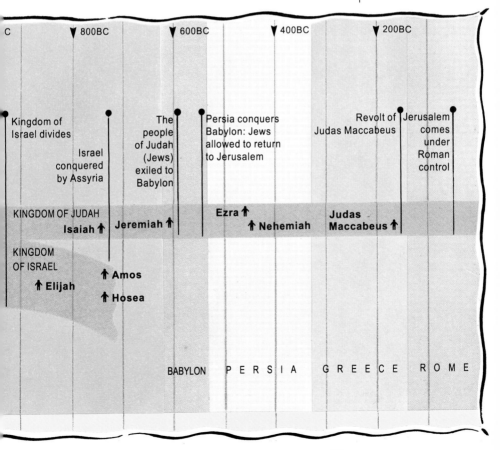

C ▼ 800BC ▼ 600BC ▼ 400BC ▼ 200BC

Kingdom of Israel divides

Israel conquered by Assyria

The people of Judah (Jews) exiled to Babylon

Persia conquers Babylon: Jews allowed to return to Jerusalem

Revolt of Judas Maccabeus

Jerusalem comes under Roman control

KINGDOM OF JUDAH
Isaiah ⬆ | Jeremiah ⬆

Ezra ⬆
⬆ Nehemiah

Judas Maccabeus ⬆

KINGDOM OF ISRAEL
⬆ Elijah

⬆ Amos

⬆ Hosea

BABYLON   P E R S I A   G R E E C E   R O M E

6

Speaking for God

● ● ● ● ● ● ● ● ● ● ● ● ●

Sometimes today we speak of someone as a 'prophet'. We may mean that they have a gift for seeing how the future will unfold. Or that they have something to say which challenges the assumptions and values of our society. We may take little notice of them. Yet deep down we suspect that there is truth in what they say. There were prophets in Israel like that.

God had high hopes for his people. He longed for them to walk wholeheartedly in the way that was best for them. But constantly they got side-tracked. Many were attracted to the nature worship of neighbouring peoples, which made no moral demands on them and positively encouraged sexual laxity. Many, especially the more wealthy, lived for themselves rather than for their community, following the rituals of worship but being unjust to the poor. They lost sight of their calling to be an example to other nations of how God wanted people to live.

The prophets were God's agents through whom he appealed to them to get back on the right track. They spoke words of criticism and encouragement, of hope and warning. They were mostly 'outsiders' who had no official position in the state or in the religious establishment. But they had an intense vision of the sickness at the heart of society. And they suffered for their outspokenness.

Small groups of followers preserved their words in writing, and these now form the last part of the Old Testament. The order in which the prophetic books appear bears no relation to the order in which they lived. Three of the earliest ones were Amos, Hosea and Isaiah.

God and politics

The Old Testament story took place against a background of ambition and power, war and politics.

Worried about the strength of the nations around them, the people of Israel urged Samuel to appoint for them a king 'such as all the other nations have' (1 Samuel 8:5). First Saul and then David became kings of Israel, and it became a military power to be reckoned with.

King Solomon, David's son, was famous for his foreign alliances, his building schemes and his extravagant lifestyle. Forced labour was the price the people paid for his achievements.

When he died the question bubbled to the surface: would his son Rehoboam continue Solomon's oppression, or would he learn a different way to rule? The story is told in 1 Kings 11:41—12:20.

When representatives of the Israelite tribes met to affirm Rehoboam's kingship, one of them, whose name was Jeroboam, said: 'Your father put a heavy yoke on us, but now lighten the harsh labour and the heavy yoke he put on us and we will serve you.'

Rehoboam consulted two sets of advisers. His older advisers knew that there was another way of exercising power: 'If today you will be a servant to these people, they will always be your servants.' But his brash young contemporaries urged even greater oppression.

They won the day, and the fortunes of the nation were changed for ever. Rehoboam increased his tyranny and Jeroboam led a successful rebellion against him. Aiming at despotic control, Rehoboam lost most of his subjects.

From then on there were two kingdoms—Israel in the north, ruled by Jeroboam and his successors, and Judah in the south, ruled by Rehoboam and his descendants. Conflict between them rumbled on till there was little left to fight about, and they in turn fell victim to the superpowers of Assyria and Babylon.

Political power can be used to oppress people and promote injustice. Or it can be used to serve people and to build a just and tolerant community. The Old Testament political commentators were clear about which approach God favoured; the fall of both Israel and Judah was unmistakeably linked to their injustice.

Amos speaks to those who are comfortable while others suffer injustice.

Amos lived around 750BC, when the northern kingdom of Israel was separated from the southern kingdom, Judah. A shepherd from Judah, he went to prophesy in Israel. No wonder the people of the north called him an interfering busybody when he started denouncing their religious and economic life!

He warned them that God was unimpressed by all their religious worship whilst their daily lives were full of injustice. He warned them that the future which they saw so filled with hope was in fact laden with doom for them. And so it was. In 722BC the Assyrians conquered Israel and took the leading citizens into exile.

The message of Amos undermines the comfortable assumption that we have a right to an ever-increasing standard of living, whether or not we act with justice and compassion towards others.

Hosea's message of God's love for his disobedient people was echoed in his own reconciliation with his unfaithful wife.

Hosea spoke in Israel at about the same time. He focused on the problem which underlay the corruption of the nation's life—its turning away from God. Having himself married an unfaithful wife, he had special insight into how God felt about Israel's 'adultery'. From his own experience of being guided by God to seek out his wife and remake the marriage, he spoke of God's forgiving love for Israel.

Hosea's deep insight into God's care for humanity didn't lead him to be sentimental about it or to take it for granted. Knowing the lengths to which God's love would go, he warned all the more urgently of the pain which follows rejection of it.

Isaiah showed the kings of his day how closely God and politics were linked.

Isaiah lived a generation later in Jerusalem, capital of the southern kingdom. At that time the threat which Assyria posed to the northern kingdom spelt danger for Judah also. One day in the temple he had a breathtaking vision of God's greatness and holiness, which shaped his view of the nation and its prospects.

He denounced in Judah similar sins to those found by Amos in Israel. All such injustice and inhumanity was a

[The word of the Lord] is in my heart like a burning fire, shut up in my bones. I am weary of holding it in; indeed, I cannot.

JEREMIAH 20: 9

Jeremiah—prophet of crisis

Jeremiah was a prophet for forty turbulent years (from 626BC until after the destruction of Jerusalem in 587). The mighty empires of Assyria and Egypt were on the wane, and Babylon was rising fast. Three episodes in Jeremiah's life will give a picture of his career.

Scene 1: about 609BC Assyria's empire had been swallowed up by that of Babylon, and Judah's relations with Egypt were not friendly. But the people who ought to be worried were not over-concerned. Surely the God who had delivered Jerusalem from Sennacherib in 701BC would do the same again? After all, he would not allow his temple to come to harm.

Jeremiah addressed people at the temple gate as they came to worship: 'Do not trust in deceptive words and say, "The temple of the Lord, the temple of the Lord, the temple of the Lord!"' The genuine trust in God of a century before had now become just a slogan. The very people who came flooding to the temple kept their real enthusiasm for the Canaanite nature gods. And the nation was morally bankrupt.

Jeremiah's career as a prophet and as a human being nearly ended there and then. But thanks to a friend he was saved from attack by the crowd (Jeremiah 7 and 26).

Scene 2: 604BC It was a day of fasting, ordered because of the national crisis. Babylonian armies threatened the land, and all Jeremiah's earlier warnings of invasion now seemed plausible after all. Jeremiah asked his secretary Baruch to write on a scroll all his previous prophecies and read them to the people at the temple.

King Jehoiakim, sitting by the fire in his winter palace, got wind of what had happened. The scroll was brought and read to him. After three or four columns had been read, the king grabbed the scroll, cut off the part that had been read and threw it on the fire. Section by section the whole scroll was read, cut and burnt to cinders.

When Jeremiah got news of this, he asked Baruch to write it all out again. The prophet's words must be preserved, so that in due course people could judge for themselves whether he had truly understood the mind of God.

Scene 3: 587BC Babylonian armies surrounded Jerusalem. Jeremiah was under house arrest, to stop his gloomy messages depressing the people any further. His cousin Hanamel arrived wondering if Jeremiah would like to buy a field at Anathoth.

This was Jeremiah's home village, a few miles north of Jerusalem. To own a field there was a nice idea. There was only one problem. The whole area was swarming with Babylonian soldiers. Yet Jeremiah solemnly weighed out seventeen shekels of silver and had the correct legal documents drawn up.

Now people had a different reason for thinking that Jeremiah was crazy. Why should a prophet of doom buy land occupied by the enemy who was about to bring utter ruin to Jerusalem and force its people into exile?

But it was an act of hope by a man convinced that beyond judgment lay a new beginning. The exile would last for a generation, but what then? 'This is what the Lord Almighty, the God of Israel, says: Houses, fields and vineyards will again be bought in this land' (Jeremiah 32).

In this act of hope, as in his earlier warnings of destruction, Jeremiah turned out be be right. If the value of a prophet is measured by his success in persuading his audience, Jeremiah was a failure. But if being a prophet is about listening to God and telling others what God has said, whatever the personal consequences, then he was one of the greatest.

denial of the relationship the people claimed with the holy God. He warned Ahaz the king that his desperate attempts to make alliances with one foreign nation against others would recoil on his head. His message was, 'Trust God, even when times are dark. You are safer with him than with any amount of playing at power politics.'

The prophets continually called God's people back to holiness and justice.

Isaiah found a more responsive king in Ahaz's son and successor Hezekiah. When the Assyrian emperor Sennacherib invaded Judah in 701BC God promised him through Isaiah, 'He will not enter this city or shoot an arrow here . . . I will defend this city and save it, for my sake and for the sake of David my servant'. And so it proved. Most of Sennacherib's huge army was destroyed by a plague and he withdrew without delay.

Other parts of Isaiah's prophecy warned that God would punish the people of Judah with exile if they didn't abandon their ungodly ways. But beyond exile there was a new beginning for a nation trusting God which would bring blessing to the nations around it.

Chapters 40–55 probably don't come from Isaiah himself but from a later prophet while the people of Judah were in exile in Babylon. His message responds with hope to the agonized questions they must have asked:

Had God been defeated by the gods of Babylon?

No, replied the prophet, he was the creator of all things, more powerful than any other force in the universe.

Had he let Judah down by allowing them to suffer like this?

No, they had let him down, and their exile was the consequence of their unfaithfulness.

Had he abandoned them for ever?

No—he was about to restore them to Judah.

God's miracles of deliverance aren't confined to the past. If he enabled the Israelites to escape from Egypt he will arrange a new 'exodus' to bring them again to the Promised Land. There they will rediscover their role as his servant and renew their mission to bring light to the world.

Isaiah 55–66 reflects the time when many of the exiles had already returned to Judah. Faced with the enormous task of rebuilding their society, they needed all the encouragement which this prophet could give. He offered a vision not only of a new Jerusalem but of a universe transformed.

But such a glorious future doesn't come without the cooperation of God's people. The holy God requires a holy people. As bluntly and as passionately as Amos, this prophet described the kind of life in society which God demands.

The Messiah

The Jews believed that God had begun to free his people through his action in the lives of Abraham and Moses. He was committed to them and was going to carry his plan through to the end.

But they knew that life was often painful and unfair—not at all as it should be if God was totally in charge of things. They knew too that the kings who were meant to rule them well were often unjust and unfaithful to God. There was little sign that a world of perfect justice and peace would come through them. So how were things going to change?

Prophets brought the vision of an ideal future king, a descendant of the great King David who would be called 'Wonderful Counsellor, Mighty God, Everlasting Father, Prince of Peace'. When he came he would 'proclaim peace to the nations'. The earth would be 'full of the knowledge of the Lord as the waters cover the sea' (Isaiah 9:2–7; 11:1–9; Micah 5:2; Zechariah 9:9–13).

Later this expected bringer of peace and freedom was called 'the Messiah'. This is simply a Hebrew word meaning 'the anointed one'. Kings were anointed—they had oil smeared or poured on their heads—as a sign that they were appointed by God to their role of leadership among God's people.

The deliverer for whom the Jews longed was to be a kingly figure, descended from David. He would be God's way of bringing to the world God's triumph over evil, suffering and death.

Was all this just wishful thinking? Were they inventing a hope of better times to come merely to help them cope with their present distress?

We might draw that conclusion, except for two things. First, their hope for the future was not simply invented out of nothing. It was based on their past experience of God, which gave them confidence that he wouldn't leave his work unfinished.

Secondly, Christians believe that Jesus, 'great David's greater son', is the Messiah who was promised. We no longer have to hope for someone to turn up. Through Jesus God has already responded to the longings of his people. The Old Testament story is an unfinished story. But beyond it lies its completion in the story of Jesus told in the New Testament.

The thing that hit me between the eyes were the Messianic prophecies from the part of the Scriptures Christians call the Old Testament, our territory, the Tanach. I was familiar with the hit stories—Moses, David, Solomon, Esther—but I'd never read or heard these bits before. Or that Messiah had been prophesied. I'd seen various quotes on Christmas cards. Things like 'For to us a child is born, to us a son is given; and the government will be upon his shoulder, and his name will be called "Wonderful counsellor, Mighty God, Everlasting Father, Prince of Peace,"'. But I'd always thought they came from the New Testament. Now I realized that was in Isaiah 9:6. One of ours!

Helen Shapiro, singer

7

Poetry and wisdom

● ● ● ● ● ● ● ● ● ● ● ● ● ●

There are times when we feel like singing for joy or shouting in anger at things that happen to us. There are times when we are in deep despair. There are times when we are full of doubt, when we long to ask God why things are as they are.

The Old Testament has space for all these emotions. The fact that they are included there suggests that God gives us permission to express them. He doesn't want people to pretend that they are feeling great and are full of faith when they are not. He expects people to be honest with him—and with each other.

Proverbs, Job and Ecclesiastes are called 'wisdom books', because they express the thoughts of the wise about how life works. Unlike other books we have looked at, their ideas aren't closely tied in with the life and history of Israel. They deal with questions about what it means to be human. And they sometimes draw on the teachings of the wise in other countries such as Babylon and Egypt. A true insight is a true insight, wherever it comes from.

Proverbs deals with everyday experiences of life. It is a collection of short sayings which often make us smile. They invite us to reflect on our own attitudes and actions and to ask: Is this wisdom or folly? For instance:

Like a gold ring in a pig's snout is a beautiful woman who shows no discretion.

PROVERBS 11:22

The lazy man says, 'There is a lion outside. I shall be killed if I go out on the street!'

PROVERBS 22:13

If a man loudly blesses his neighbour early in the morning, it will be taken as a curse.

PROVERBS 27:14

The value of all this is that it makes religious people keep their feet on the ground. Those people who are so spiritual that they lack common sense need a daily dose of Proverbs.

If Proverbs was the only wisdom book, we might conclude that Israel's wise men were a rather optimistic bunch of people who hadn't faced up to the dark side of life. But the book of Job breathes a very different atmosphere. One of the finest poems in the whole of world literature, it asks why innocent people suffer.

Job is a good man overwhelmed by the most extreme suffering. Three friends come to 'comfort' him. 'Your suffering must be due to sins which you have secretly committed. You can't be as good as we all thought. So ask God's forgiveness, and maybe he will restore you.'

This is as helpful to Job as a tin-opener to a drowning man. In the end God himself speaks. Yet he doesn't give a straight answer to Job's question, 'Why am I suffering?' He says, in effect, 'Will you trust me to run the world according to my wisdom?'

The book of Proverbs shows God's wisdom at work in everyday life.

Job takes a straight look at the problem of undeserved suffering.

The Psalms—many responses to the one God

What kind of God did the people of the Old Testament believe in? Because the Psalms express Israel's response to God in varied circumstances, they show us what God meant to them.

God is Creator of the whole world. He delights in it and wants humanity to enjoy it and care for it.

How many are your works, O Lord!
In wisdom you made them all;
the earth is full of your creatures.
Psalm 104:24

God acts in history, especially in the experience of his people Israel.

He saved them for his name's sake,
to make his mighty power known.
He rebuked the Red Sea, and it dried up;
he led them through the depths as through a desert.
Psalm 106:8–9

God desires to show mercy and forgiveness.

The Lord is compassionate and gracious,
slow to anger, abounding in love . . .
He does not treat us as our sins deserve
or repay us according to our iniquities.
Psalm 103:8, 10

But he opposes those who resist his purpose, especially those who oppress the powerless and deny justice to the poor. He holds people to account for their lives.

Rise up, O Judge of the earth;
pay back to the proud what they deserve.
How long will the wicked, O Lord,
how long will the wicked be jubilant?
Psalm 94:2–3

God guides his people through the Bible.

Your word is a lamp to my feet
and a light for my path.
Psalm 119:105

God draws close to those who bring to him their needs and anxieties.

The Lord is my shepherd, I shall not be in want...
Even though I walk through the valley of the shadow of death,
I will fear no evil, for you are with me;
your rod and your staff, they comfort me.
Psalm 23:1, 4

Though God seems sometimes not to protect his people and their faith is severely strained, he remains their source of hope. They would rather live with the question why he seems to be hidden from them than abandon trust in him.

How long will the enemy mock you, O God?
Will the foe revile your name for ever?
Why do you hold back your hand, your right hand?...
But you, O God, are my king from of old;
You bring salvation upon the earth.
Psalm 74:10–11

God will one day set all things right and establish his rule over all the world.

He comes to judge the earth.
He will judge the world in righteousness
and the peoples in his truth.
Psalm 96:13

There is no tidy answer to why suffering affects the innocent. But beyond the anger and the questions we may discover God's presence. He isn't remote, blaming us for our wrongdoing. He is waiting to be discovered as the friend who stands beside us in our suffering.

Ecclesiastes ('the philosopher') perhaps rings more bells in our day than any other book of the Bible. Its author seems to hover between faith and doubt, between enjoyment of life and puzzlement about life's meaning.

'Utterly meaningless!', he says, 'Everything is meaningless!'. He has tried all the normal routes to find satisfaction and meaning to life—pleasure, money, philosophy, hard work, power over others. But there is always a craving for more. And sooner or later death puts a full stop to everyone's life. What meaning is left then? Yet at the same time he feels that life is a gift of God, and that to obey God's commandments is 'the whole duty of mankind'.

Like many people today this writer stumbles between these two reactions. He feels that the meaning of life is always out of his reach, and that death mocks so much of human achievement, and yet that it is right to enjoy the good things of life.

Perhaps there is no real answer to his questions, unless death itself can be conquered. But that is a question to which the New Testament offers a fuller answer than can be found within the Old Testament.

The Psalms are the hymn-book and prayer-book of

The book of Ecclesiastes echoes the modern dilemma of trying to find meaning in a contradictory world.

The Psalms offer us words for every human situation and emotion.

> *I found great solace in reading the Psalms. The anguished suffering mind that had created them and had cried out to God in his suffering reflected much of our own condition. Exhausted with profound questions and never finding an answer, we took relief in devotional moments.*
>
> Brian Keenan, held hostage in Lebanon for four and a half years

the Jews. In biblical times the sound of their words filled the temple in Jerusalem, and they continue to be sung by Jews and Christians today. They show us a lot about how the Israelites expressed their faith and hope, their thanks and fears to God. Different kinds of psalms provide words for different needs and occasions.

There is variety here to speak to every human emotion and situation. The book of Psalms can suggest to us what to say to God when we have no words for what we are feeling.

They show us that it is all right to question God, to throw at him our anger and our frustration. They show how we can take encouragement in a present crisis by recalling how God has dealt with past crises. They remind us too that even when we feel most alone we can be part of a community of faith.

Even when we feel most alone, we can be part of a community of faith.

The Old Testament on trial

● ● ● ● ● ● ● ● ● ● ● ● ● ● ●

A book which aims to introduce people to the Old Testament shouldn't hide the difficulties which are there. Here are three issues which often puzzle people.

How does God speak?

Stories in the Bible often include phrases such as 'God said to Abraham'. This presents a problem to modern readers.

Should we conclude that God had a special way of getting his message over to people in those days, which he doesn't use today? Or that the biblical writers were simply imagining that God spoke to people?

Today God might speak through a friend's advice or through a certain situation. Sometimes there may be a growing conviction over a period of time that we should make some major change in our lives.

At other times, words from the Bible can make a strong impression. They seem to come as a special message from God about our own situation. And I have met people who believed so strongly that God was speaking to them about something that it really felt as though they could *hear* his voice.

God spoke to people in Old Testament times in similar ways. The writers' vivid way of story-telling led them to write simply, 'God said to Abraham...'. But those simple words probably reflect the variety of experiences which believers in God have today.

The God whom Christians worship today is the same God who called Abraham. And he wants to tell us, too, how to live.

But when we try to listen to what God is saying we are often not sure whether it is really him speaking. Maybe I feel he is calling me to speak in public. But is that really his will for me, or is it just because I enjoy talking?

It takes time and experience to be sure that God is really speaking in a particular way. The Old Testament writers had both. Those who wrote the story of Abraham were collecting memories passed on through generations of storytellers.

By the time they wrote they couldn't know exactly how God's extraordinary call had come to Abraham, and how he was persuaded to leave security behind and set off for Canaan.

But they knew he had made that journey. And they could see with hindsight that it really had been a journey planned and guided by God. They could see that it was the start of a continuing story in which God was guiding his people and showing them his loving purpose for the world.

God spoke to people in Old Testament times as he speaks to us today.

Why is the Old Testament so full of blood and guts?

Our world is weary of war and the monstrous treatment of men and women which goes with it. So it isn't surprising that we find it distasteful to read so often of

The Old Testament world is not so different from our own—nations still struggle for power, killing the innocent in the process.

wars and violence, particularly in the historical books of the Old Testament.

But perhaps that is the place to begin thinking about the problem. The fighting is there because the Old Testament world wasn't so different from our own. Then, as now, nations wrestled for power over each other, abusing their fellow human beings in the process.

And it was inevitable that the Israelites would be caught up in this because their land was vulnerable to invasion from all directions. From ancient times until the present day the armies of Egypt, Assyria, Babylon, Greece, Rome, the Arabs and the Turks have seen control of this land as the key to control of the Middle East.

The real problem is not that war figures so much in the stories, but that the Israelites *used* war to establish themselves in Canaan under Joshua's leadership. And that—according to the Old Testament—God *told* them to kill all the inhabitants of the Canaanite cities which they conquered. What can be said about that?

◆ **When they came to Canaan the Israelites themselves were landless refugees.**

Only people who have been in that situation can really understand what it's like to lack the security of home and land.

◆ **The reason given for such drastic treatment of conquered Canaanites was that if they survived they might lead the Israelites to abandon the true God and engage in the perverted worship of Canaanite gods.**

At a critical period of their history, maybe the Israelites were simply not strong enough in their faith to be able to cope with the Canaanites and their religion.

◆ **The Old Testament writers also took for granted that God uses the events of war to pass judgment on wicked people.**

The same book of Deuteronomy warns that the Israelites themselves would be the victims of defeat in war if they turned away from God and his protection—a prophecy which was ultimately fulfilled. In the long run it is right, not might, which prevails in the affairs of nations.

◆ **The Old Testament lays down limits on what is permitted in war.**

These constraints contrasted sharply with the 'anything goes' approach of some neighbouring countries. For instance, if laying siege to a city the Israelites could cut down trees to build siege works, but could not take fruit-bearing trees. Out of respect for life, this law forbade the kind of ruthless destruction which the Assyrians later made famous and which has become such a horrifying part of modern warfare.

◆ **Out of Israel's later experience of defeat in war came the realization that God's way for his people was not one of military victory.**

In Isaiah 40–55 (especially chapter 53) Israel is pictured as God's servant. This servant is to be gentle and, when necessary, to accept suffering. God's purpose for the world comes about not when his people try to solve their problems through force, but when they realize that out of suffering he can bring life for the world.

The description of the 'suffering servant' in the book of Isaiah foreshadows God's plan of bringing life for the world out of suffering.

Isn't it all fairy stories?

For many people the Old Testament is a collection of stories on the same level as Father Christmas or the tooth fairy.

But different parts of the Old Testament are different types of literature. They need approaching in different ways.

Some books, such as Proverbs or Psalms, make no claim to be historical. The story of Jonah and the 'whale'

Discovered in 1880, Hezekiah's water tunnel was originally built to ensure a fresh water supply to Jerusalem in case of siege.

Also discovered over 100 years ago, is this cylinder which dates from 536BC. It records how Cyrus took Babylon and freed people to return to their original homes.

Archaeological discoveries such as these help to authenticate events from this part of the Bible.

was probably never intended as an account of historical events. It is a story which through humour and irony makes its point about God's love even for Israel's enemies.

The very beginning of Genesis takes us back to the beginnings of time, illustrating the nature of human experience and revealing profound truths about our relationship with God. But when we reach Abraham in Genesis 12 we begin to be in touch with a historical world known to us through the findings of archaeology.

Abraham and his family had names common in the world at that time. Their lifestyle and customs fit with many things we now know about the Middle East around 1800BC. For instance, Abraham bought a field in which was a cave where he could bury his wife Sarah. The method of sale described in Genesis 23 is also known from other documents of the time.

None of this proves that the story of Abraham happened as Genesis describes it. But it makes it unlikely that the story was simply invented many years later.

When we come to the historical books there are certain points at which the Bible's record can be compared with the records of Middle Eastern rulers and other archaeological discoveries. Here are some examples.

Sennacherib was emperor of Assyria from 705 to 681BC. His official records, found by archaeologists in his capital Nineveh, report his siege of Jerusalem in 701, when Hezekiah was king of Judah:

As to Hezekiah the Jew, he did not submit to my yoke. I laid siege to forty-six of his strong cities, walled forts and countless small villages in the vicinity and conquered them . . . Himself I made a prisoner in Jerusalem, his royal residence, like a bird in a cage . . .

The Bible's account is in 2 Kings 18–19. It is obviously the same event, though 2 Kings 19 also tells how the city was delivered. Sennacherib naturally glossed over the fact

The beginning of Genesis answers profound questions about God, human nature and the way the world is. Later books of the Old Testament chronicle the history of nations, but still from God's point of view.

The Bible's record is frequently confirmed by archaeological findings.

Like all historians, the Old Testament writers interpreted the events they described. Their descriptions are borne out by other sources of the time, though not always with the same interpretation!

that he didn't actually capture Jerusalem. Like any emperor, he wanted to present even his failures and disappointments as successes!

One important reason why Hezekiah was able to hold out against the siege was that he built a tunnel to bring water inside the city walls from the Gihon spring, which was outside. This detail is reported in 2 Kings 20:20.

In 1880 two boys swimming in the Pool of Siloam found their way through a small passage into a tunnel cut in the rock. It was discovered that the tunnel wound its way through 500 metres of limestone to the Gihon spring. And inside the tunnel was a Hebrew inscription from Hezekiah's time, explaining how workmen beginning from each end had met in the middle. You can still wade through this tunnel today.

One hundred and forty-two years after Hezekiah's reign, when the Jews had been in exile in Babylon for half a century, the Persian king Cyrus conquered Babylon and permitted the Jews to return home. This is referred to in Isaiah 40 and 45, and described in Ezra 1. Cyrus' own account is preserved on the Cyrus Cylinder, an inscription written on clay. Referring to the areas from which captive peoples came, he wrote: 'I gathered together all their inhabitants and restored them to their dwellings.' Here again we see the biblical account confirmed.

There are many points where Old Testament history can't be checked with other ancient records. There are still many gaps in our knowledge. And at some points

> *Archaeology can neither prove the Bible nor disprove its claims, for they are about God. But as all its discoveries increase our knowledge of the world in which the Bible was written, so they enable its distinctive religious message to stand out more boldly.*
>
> Alan Millard, archaeologist

the findings of archaeology raise questions about the biblical record rather than confirming it. But there is enough confirmation from other sources to allow us to say that the historical value of the biblical accounts is always to be taken seriously.

Like all historians, the Old Testament writers interpreted the meaning of historical events in the light of what they thought was important. But there is every reason to believe that their historical writings describe real events, not just the creations of their imagination.

Archaeology cannot prove or disprove the Bible's claims about God, but it can provide a background to biblical history.

9

Reading the
Old Testament

●●●●●●●●●●●●●●●

Not many people begin at Genesis and read
straight through to the end of the Old
Testament! We need a varied diet. And it isn't
always easy to build bridges between words
written two or three thousand years ago and
our own lives today.

It's a good idea to begin with a book which has plenty of
stories, like Genesis. You can read it a chapter at a time,
or in longer chunks as you would a novel. Then perhaps
read some of the shorter books—the prophecy of Amos
or of Micah, the story of Ruth or of Nehemiah. Psalms
and Proverbs are two books which can be dipped into a
bit at a time, since there is no connecting theme or story
between the chapters.

It's helpful to ask certain questions when we are
reading a passage. This may seem complicated at first.
It's rather like learning to drive. When you begin you
think, how will I remember all these different things that
I have to do at the same time? But gradually it becomes
second nature and you do the right things almost
without thinking. With a little practice, we learn

Studying a passage

Let's try out some of these questions on one biblical story— the story of King David's affair with Bathsheba (2 Samuel 11:1-12:14).

What kind of a book?
2 Samuel is one of the historical books which show God working out his purpose through the history of his people. So we shouldn't look for deep meaning in every verse, but see it as part of a longer story of God's dealings with Israel.

What did it mean?
Obviously, the narrative is set in the life of David, about 1000BC. It is tempting for us to see the story as a warning about adultery. That theme is there, but it isn't the main purpose of a historical book. It is part of the story of how

God overcame the worst weaknesses of his servants in order to fulfil his purpose.

How can I apply this meaning and put it into practice?
Viewed in this way, the story offers us encouragement, and a reason to celebrate God's amazing love. If he could work through David despite his failure, there's hope for us!

What does the New Testament add?
The fact that David was the ancestor of Jesus, God's Messiah, underlines this point about God's love. He never says, 'I told you so', and abandons us to the mess we have created. His love is always looking for fresh ways to achieve his plan to bless the whole of humanity.

naturally to ask the right questions of the passages we read.

What kind of a book is it?

You read a history book in a different way from the instruction manual for a CD player. And different kinds of biblical books need different approaches.

When we read how God shaped the life of someone such as David or Ruth, we can see how he can speak to our own situation. But if we are reading laws in Deuteronomy, we will look for instructions about how to live. In a historical book such as 2 Kings we will look mainly to see how God's purpose for Israel was worked out, and what that might suggest for God's work in the world today.

What did it mean then?

Because the Bible comes from a very different world from our own, we should try to be conscious of the historical context of what we are reading.

If we know, for example, that Amos was prophesying at a time of economic growth and moral decline in the northern kingdom of Israel, shortly before its destruction, we shall make a lot more sense of his message. That's where the introduction to each biblical book which can be found in some Bibles is very helpful.

How can I apply this meaning today?

Sometimes this is easy. A psalm, for example, can immediately suggest ways of praying which are as relevant to us as to an ancient Israelite.

For a passage of the Old Testament to speak to us, we must ask the right questions.

At other times we must tread more carefully. When we read laws which can't be applied directly in our culture we may find a principle underlying the laws which is important for us.

For instance, Deuteronomy 22:8 says: 'When you build a new house, make a parapet around your roof.' This law holds builders responsible for the safety of those who use their buildings. A flat roof without a wall round it was obviously dangerous. The same principle might require that we protect workers from dangerous machinery in factories, or that traffic be barred from streets where children play.

How can I put it into practice?

The Bible is a practical book for people who are aiming to know God better and to do his will. So when we read it we will want to ask, how will this change my understanding of God? How will it help my relationship with him? What difference will it make to the way I live?

What does the New Testament add?

Often the Old Testament doesn't have the last word on a particular topic. So when we read the Old Testament on marriage, for instance, Jesus' words in the Gospels or the teaching of the New Testament letters add important new perspectives. And what the prophets say about God's future plans makes more sense when we discover how those plans are fulfilled in Jesus.

What help can I get?

No one has to struggle with the Bible all alone. In fact, the people who wrote the Old Testament would have found it strange to think that anyone should read these writings on their own. No one in those days had their own books on a shelf at home. They were too difficult and expensive to produce.

The Bible was a book of the community. It was read in the temple or studied in groups. People helped each other to understand and apply it.

Maybe you can study with a group like this. Or you can get Bible reading notes from a church or a bookshop. These will guide you through a variety of biblical books and suggest ways of understanding and putting them into practice.

Laws about situations which are specific to Old Testament times can still have underlying principles to guide us today.

Studying a theme

Sometimes we want to find out what the Old Testament says on a particular subject. Here, for example, is some of its teaching about marriage and families.

◆ **There is instruction.**

Genesis 1:27–28 suggests that God made male and female to be complementary, and that part of their role together is to have children. Genesis 2:18–25 stresses that their relationship is chiefly to provide companionship for each other. When they marry they loosen ties with their parents in order to be wholly committed to each other.

◆ **There are specific laws designed to protect marriage.**

Adultery is forbidden (Exodus 20:14), and a recently married man is excused military service (Deuteronomy 24:5). There are laws too about the respect of children for their parents (Exodus 20:12).

◆ **There are stories about the finding of a marriage partner (Genesis 24) and about love within marriage (Genesis 29–31).**

◆ There are down-to-earth proverbs about attitudes in marriage and the family (Proverbs 5:15–20; 19:13–14; 22:6).

There is a whole section on the qualities of the ideal wife (Proverbs 31:10–31), who runs her own textile business as well as managing her household and caring for her children!

◆ And there is poetry about the passionate love of a young couple (Song of Songs), from both the woman's and the man's point of view.

In ancient Israel, as in many cultures today, the family was not a small unit of two parents and two or three children. It was a wide network of relatives who supported each other through good times and bad. There was always someone to turn to when life was difficult. And single people were also part of these relationships.

The riches of the Old Testament

The Word of God is like a compass, like a map showing the routes, the way to the end. It is food for the soul and without it you are not full, but always hungry.

Thai Christian girl

Such varied material as the Old Testament offers cannot all be applied at face value in the varied cultures of the world today. And the teaching of Jesus and the New Testament revises and enriches it. But it provides the raw materials to guide us. Far from being out of date, its perspective can sometimes challenge the poverty of modern attitudes.

Through myth and poetry, history and legislation, the Old Testament does more than show us the life of a culture that has passed away. It was the Old Testament that formed Jesus' knowledge of God, and it can still speak to us about God today.

Starting with the
New Testament

The New Testament is a book about Jesus Christ. It is also a book about us, our concerns and questions.

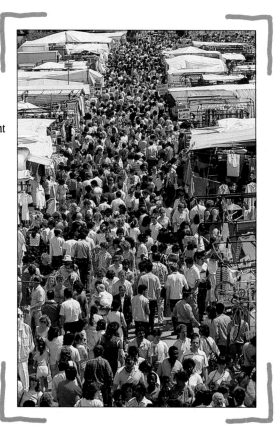

1

What's it all about?

● ● ● ● ● ● ● ● ● ● ● ● ● ● ●

Huddled together under the corrugated iron roof of a *favela* in Rio de Janeiro, twenty people of various ages are talking excitedly about the meaning of the Bible for their lives.

At a university in Siberia, 150 staff and students—most of them not Christians—are studying a passage from the New Testament and asking what it means for them.

In 1991 a man is made Archbishop of Canterbury who, as a teenager, began to go to church and 'found the worship boring but the preaching from the Bible riveting'.

What is it about the New Testament which claims such attention? How can a small book written so long ago still have such influence in the world? Why should it matter to me?

To answer these questions we must go back to Jerusalem in about AD30. Jesus, from the town of Nazareth in the north of Palestine, has gained a reputation as a prophet and miracle-worker. Some Jews have treasured the hope that he will deliver them from

The Christian Bible is divided into two parts:

The word 'testament' means 'agreement'. The Bible's first half is about the agreement God made with the people of Israel, while the second half—the New Testament— revolves around the agreement God made available to all people through the death of Jesus Christ.

the occupying armies of Rome. To his closest followers he is 'the Messiah'—the one specially sent to bring God's presence and his blessings close to people in a new way.

But the religious authorities, worried that his popularity may undermine their own position, have joined forces with the Roman governor Pontius Pilate to get rid of him. Pilate has sentenced him to be horribly killed by crucifixion. Jesus' followers as well as his enemies have watched him die, and his body has been taken away for burial.

Now it is Sunday morning, two days after the crucifixion. Some of Jesus' followers come as mourners to his tomb. To their astonishment, they find that the huge stone which sealed the tomb entrance has been rolled away, and the tomb itself is empty. And then Jesus, in a series of appearances over several weeks, shows himself to them unmistakably alive! He has risen from death!

Jesus' resurrection meant for his followers—and means for us—that he is alive for ever, available to bring God close to men and women

The event of that Sunday transformed his followers' lives. Jesus' risen life, his resurrection, meant for them—and means for us—that he is alive for ever and available to bring God close to men and women.

The New Testament is a book about Jesus Christ. Without his resurrection it would not exist. It is also a book about us, our concerns and our questions:

- ◆ **What is the purpose of life?**

- ◆ **Is it possible to know God in a personal way?**

- ◆ **How can we live so as to make a better world for our children?**

- ◆ **Why am I such a mixture of hopes and failures, idealism and selfishness?**

- ◆ **Why doesn't God do something about all the suffering in the world?**

> *I went to the Commonwealth Games in 1986 in a bit of a turmoil, wondering what life was really about. As I went into the room there was a Good News Bible on my bed. I picked it up and started reading it. I met a character in there I'd never met before, and Jesus Christ challenged me to think about what the real meaning of life was. And I liked the things he had to say. Most importantly he seemed to respect me for who I was as a person, and I was challenged. Nine months later I asked him to make himself more real to me, and my faith grew from there.*
>
> Kriss Akabusi, Olympic athlete

The New Testament was written over a period of about fifty years by a variety of different people. In this sense it is a fully human book. The difference is that God chose its writers and inspired them to write in such a way that their words revealed the character and the plans of God.

Through the words of the New Testament, the risen Jesus speaks to us about ourselves and about his purpose for us. But how are we to hear and understand what he says? Where should we begin to read?

The first thing to notice is that the New Testament isn't one book, like a novel or a biography. It's a collection of twenty-seven books, written in different styles by a variety of authors.

And there's no better place to start than with the writings of the man who wrote more pages of the New Testament than anyone else. His name is Luke.

The New Testament isn't one book, like a novel or a biography. It's a collection of twenty-seven books, written in different styles by a variety of authors.

2

The story that had to be told

● ● ● ● ● ● ● ● ● ● ● ● ● ●

Luke is one of four people in the first-century church—the first people who became followers of Jesus—who wrote 'Gospels'. We tend to think of them as biographies of Jesus. But what strange biographies!

They tell us almost nothing about Jesus' life before he was thirty years old. They don't tell us what he looked like. They tell us very little about his inner thoughts and reasons for doing things. They spend a surprising amount of space on the last week of his life and the circumstances of his death. Why? Because they aren't simply biographies but Gospels! The word 'gospel' means 'good news'.

The Gospels tell the story of Jesus not just to give us interesting facts about a historical person. They tell it so that we may discover good news about how Jesus can make a life-changing impact on us!

This is what makes Luke's book, and the other Gospels, different from any other book. He tells stories about what Jesus did and said in Palestine around AD30 so that we get an impression of what kind of person Jesus was, and why he had such an amazing effect on people.

The story of Jesus' life was so dramatic, so life-changing, that his followers made sure that it was recorded.

But, remember, Luke believes in the risen Jesus—the Jesus who is alive today. So whenever he tells a story about the Jesus who taught and brought fresh hope and healed and forgave people in Palestine, he is saying at the same time that the same Jesus can do the same things for people anywhere, any time.

That's what makes his book good news! That's why we read it today and expect it to affect our lives.

It didn't occur to Jesus' followers to write down an account of his life immediately after his death and resurrection. Most of them were not bookish people. Stories about him were remembered and passed on to others in the course of preaching the new message. Where people don't have books to rely on, their memories remain amazingly vivid and accurate.

But about thirty years after the resurrection, when many of the people who had known Jesus in Palestine

How to find chapter and verse

If you wanted someone to find a particular passage in a modern book such as Graham Greene's novel *Our Man in Havana*, you would simply tell them to look up page 73, or whichever page you have in mind. With the Bible, a method of providing references was devised which can be confusing if you are not used to it.

To make it easy to refer to particular sentences in the Bible, each book is divided into chapters, and each chapter is again divided into verses. So 1 Corinthians 13:4 (or 1 Cor. 13:4) means Paul's first letter to the Corinthian church, chapter 13, verse 4. John 3:16–21 means John's Gospel, chapter 3, verses 16–21. 2 John 12 means the second letter of John, verse 12 (this short letter is not divided into separate chapters).

The contents page of any Bible or New Testament lists the books in the order in which they appear, and shows the page on which each one begins.

The first letter to the
　Corinthian church
　　　　chapter
　　　　　verse

1 Corinthians 13 : 4

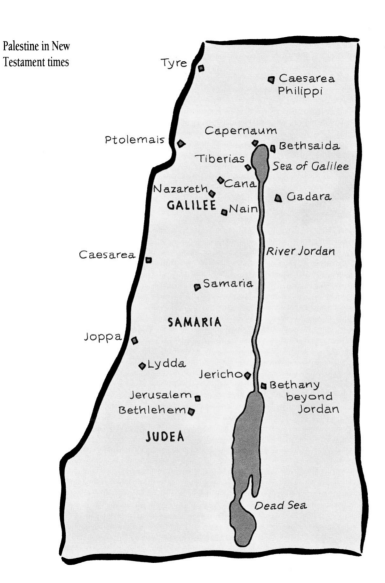

Palestine in New
Testament times

were at the end of their lives, Christians began to want an accurate written record of his life to pass on to the next generation. One of these writers was a Greek called Luke.

We know little about Luke, except that he was a doctor and a friend of the apostle Paul (see Paul's mention of him in his letter to the Colossians). He is probably the only non-Jewish (Gentile) writer in the New Testament.

The word 'apostle' comes from the Greek word for 'messenger'. Jesus' closest followers were called his 'apostles' because they spread the message of his resurrection, but Paul became known as 'apostle to the Gentiles' because he told non-Jewish people (Gentiles) about Jesus.

Luke wrote two books—the Gospel according to Luke, and the Acts of the Apostles. The second of these we shall come to later, but let's look first at his Gospel.

It will be helpful to have a copy of the New Testament, or of the whole Bible, handy. It is available in various modern translations. I recommend the New International Version or the Good News Bible.

Luke opens with a statement about why he is writing.

Many have undertaken to draw up an account of the things that have been fulfilled among us, just as they were handed down to us by those who from the first were eyewitnesses and servants of the word. Therefore, since I myself have carefully investigated everything from the beginning, it seemed good also to me to write an orderly account for you, most excellent Theophilus, so that you may know the certainty of the things you have been taught.
LUKE 1:1–4

He tells us here that others have already written about Jesus, drawing on the stories constantly used in the church's preaching. He tells us that he himself has done some careful research to check out the story he is about to relate. He dedicates his book to someone called Theophilus, probably a new convert to Christianity, who has promised to meet the cost of producing Luke's two books.

And Luke's purpose in writing is to bring home to Theophilus the 'certainty' or the 'full truth' of what he has so far been taught about Jesus. Naturally, his book has a special attraction for people exploring Christian faith for the first time.

After that he launches into his story. And there's no better way to find out what he says than to read it for yourself. To read it in three manageable sections, I suggest dividing it like this:

◆ Luke 1:1–9:50
   Jesus' birth and his life and teaching in Galilee

◆ Luke 9:51–19:27
   Jesus' journey to Jerusalem

◆ Luke 19:28–24:53
   Jesus' life, death and resurrection in Jerusalem

But to get the flavour of what Luke especially wants to tell us about Jesus, we'll dip into five episodes in his story.

Luke wrote down what he knew about Jesus to tell the 'full truth' to his contemporaries. What he tells is as relevant today as it was all those years ago.

3

Headline events from Luke's Gospel

● ● ● ● ● ● ● ● ● ● ● ● ● ●

Luke's Gospel is the story of Jesus told in such a way as to show what his life and teaching, his death and resurrection, can mean both for Luke's first readers and for us. Its message is fresh and relevant after all these years because Jesus himself is as alive now as he was on the first Easter Day.

In five episodes from this story we can get the message of Luke's Gospel—we can find out what sort of person Jesus of Nazareth was and is.

King born in cattle shed!

Read Luke 2:1–20

We'll begin with the familiar story of Jesus' birth. Luke tells this story in a way that emphasizes three things about Jesus:

Jesus was born into a particular place in the world at a particular time in history. His birth in Bethlehem and his life in Galilee demonstrate that God is not remote from our human lives; he is involved with us.

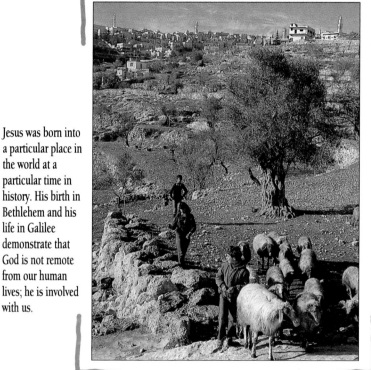

Firstly, **he sets the birth of Jesus in the context of world history**. Augustus, the Roman emperor, controlled Palestine as well as most of Europe and all the countries around the Mediterranean. Some of his subjects called him 'saviour' because he had brought peace and stability after a period of civil wars. But Luke is announcing a different kind of ruler, a different kind of saviour. And this saviour will go on affecting the whole world long after Augustus is forgotten.

Secondly, **he reports the actual birth of Jesus**. The census has made Joseph and Mary return from Nazareth, where they live, to Bethlehem, Joseph's family home. So Jesus is born in the town of his ancestor, King David.

This underlines his role as the *Messiah* (in Greek, *Christos*, Christ) expected by the Jewish people. The Old Testament led them to expect that one day a descendant of David would deliver them from all their enemies and bring in 'the kingdom of God'. Then at last there would be peace, justice and a world living in harmony with God. As we shall see, Jesus does bring the kingdom of God, but not quite in the sense that many Jews expected.

Thirdly, **Jesus' birth is announced to the world**. There are no headlines in the newspaper, no cards in the mail, but a whole chorus of angels. And the receivers of the message are not national and religious leaders, but shepherds.

Why shepherds? Just because they are ordinary people. The good news of Jesus comes first to people who have no religious qualifications, but are open to the possibility of being surprised by God.

Jesus has many titles in the New Testament. A 'saviour' is someone who rescues (or 'saves') people from danger. 'Messiah' is a Hebrew word meaning 'anointed one'. Being anointed with oil was one sign of kingship, and the Jews longed for the leader who would bring in God's kingdom. 'Christ' is the Greek word for Messiah.

Drama in Nazareth

When Jesus was thirty years old God gave him authority to begin preaching in public and healing people. In the synagogue in his home town of Nazareth there occurred one of the most dramatic incidents in the New Testament.

80

Read Luke 4:14–30

Jesus goes to the local synagogue—the building used for Jewish worship. He is invited to read from the Scriptures. He reads from the prophet Isaiah, a passage which speaks of how God will bring new hope to his people.

Then he makes the startling announcement: 'Today this scripture is fulfilled in your hearing.' What prophets glimpsed from a distance, what God's people longed for, is in their midst as he speaks. The kingdom of God has dawned because Jesus is here.

The passage from Isaiah lists several signs which would indicate the arrival of God's kingdom.

'Today,' says Jesus, 'those things are happening in what I am doing. The kingdom of God is no longer something you hope for in the future. It is something you can experience and be part of now. God has come close to you.'

'Preaching good news to the poor' sums up what Jesus was most concerned about. 'The poor' are the people who are powerless, the people written off by the political and religious establishment, the people who don't count for much in the world's eyes.

In Jesus' time they would include not only people who were short of cash but also widows, orphans, refugees, the disabled. And people who were despised because they did dirty jobs or because they benefited from the Roman occupation of Palestine. Jesus came to show God's love particularly to such people, and Luke wants the world to know about it.

When people respond to Jesus he welcomes them into a new community. Those among his disciples who have been battered by society or by circumstances are accepted and valued in a new way. Those who have been gripped by evil habits are set free by the power of his love. 'Nobodies' become 'somebodies'. Their world is turned upside down.

The Jewish Scriptures are what Christians call the Old Testament. At the synagogue service Jewish men would take turns in reading and explaining the Scriptures.

Key stages on the journey through
the New Testament

1 Jesus is born

The place: Bethlehem, a town in Judea, 10km
south of Jerusalem.

The event: it's a well-known story — no room
at the inn, shepherds, a star, wise men, a
baby born in a cattle-stall — it's the story
Christmas is made of!

The significance: There would be no New
Testament, no Christian faith without the life
which began in Bethlehem. (The event was
so significant that the world has marked time
— AD means after the birth of Jesus — from
this event onwards.)

2 Jesus begins his work

The places: Jesus began his work in Judea. But he soon went to Galilee,
where he quickly attracted followers. The centre of his activity was
Capernaum.

The events: Jesus heals people, he teaches, he gathers a band of twelve
followers, his miracles and radical teaching catch attention — not least
from the authorities.

The significance: in only three years Jesus caused a real stir — his life and
words changed people's lives. He never travelled further than 150km from
his home town, but the message he preached has since travelled the entire
world and is still changing lives 2,000 years later.

4 The early church grows

The places: the message spreads out from Jerusalem through those who witnessed the amazing events of Jesus' last weeks on earth and through followers such as Paul, who tirelessly and fearlessly declare their beliefs.

The events: persecution of Christians by the Romans, amazing stories of martyrdom, churches growing far and abroad, Christian teaching and practice tested and confirmed.

The significance: the incredible way in which the early followers of Jesus went out and spread the news about his life and teaching is testimony to the strength of their belief in him. It's hard to imagine that they would have gone out, against all the odds, and spread the word if they had had any doubts about his resurrection. That the message is alive today, that there are millions of followers of Jesus the world over, is even greater testimony to the truth of the New Testament story.

3 Put to death and raised to life

The place: Jerusalem, a site called Golgotha

The events: the Sanhedrin (the Jewish Council of Elders) convict Jesus of blasphemy but are powerless to sentence him to death; only the Roman authorities can do that. After some manoeuvring, Pilate, the Roman governor, is persuaded to carry out the sentence. Jesus is hung on a cross, between two thieves. After six hours he is dead, and is placed in a tomb cut out of a rocky hillside. A huge stone seals the entrance.

But three days later the tomb is empty and Jesus appears, alive, to many of his followers. Within two months of Jesus' crucifixion, they are boldly proclaiming that Jesus is alive. They are prepared to suffer – even die – for their beliefs.

The significance: Christianity hangs or falls on the resurrection of Jesus. It is the climax of God's rescue plan for humankind, opening up the way for us through death into eternal life with God. You can't get much more significant than that!

But the episode at Nazareth is not finished. Jesus goes on to remind hearers how it has always been God's plan to show his favour to Gentiles, not just to Jews. Old Testament prophets such as Elijah and Elisha were sent to show God's care to people outside Palestine.

'The kingdom of God has dawned in your midst,' Jesus is saying. 'You can know its blessings—but only if you'll share them with others.'

This is more than the audience can take. They rise in hostility against Jesus, because he has threatened to disturb their cosy assumption that God is more concerned about them than about anyone else.

This story sums up the pattern of Jesus' whole ministry as Luke portrays it. His mission is especially to bring to the poor the good news that they are loved and valued, and to give them new hope. The rest of Luke's Gospel will give examples of Jesus showing God's generosity to all kinds of people who were looked down on by many of his contemporaries—people with leprosy, Samaritans, tax-collectors, those whose sins shocked society.

And his second book, the Acts of the Apostles, will report how the early church reflected Jesus' concern for all such despised people. It will show especially how the church fulfilled God's plan that his love should be made known to Gentiles.

Shocking teaching

No one can respond to Jesus without being changed by him. He makes demands on his followers which stretch their imagination and test their commitment to the limit. Here is one section of his tough, down-to-earth teaching.

Read Luke 6:27–36

To get the full force of what Jesus is driving at we must ask, who did Jesus mean by 'enemies'? To his first

There were many despised groups in first-century Palestine: people with leprosy— not only infectious, but unclean by the Law's standards—tax collectors, who were seen as collaborators with the hated Roman authorities, and prostitutes. Jesus brought new hope to such people by showing them God's love. Today his followers still care about those society would rather forget.

hearers one answer would spring to mind: the Romans. How could anyone be more hated than the foreign dictator and his armies who control your country?

So we can imagine the shock and the anger when Jesus tells people to *love* the Romans. 'That's outrageous,' they say. 'That's the last thing you'll find us doing.'

'No,' Jesus replies. 'Unless we dare to do good to our enemies instead of matching hate with hate, there will never be a new world of peace and trust. We shall destroy ourselves. And remember, if you have entered the kingdom of God you are called to be like God. And he is generous to those who hate him as well as to those who love him.'

Probably when Luke's readers heard the word 'enemies' they would think of people who hate and cause trouble for the Christian community. When we hear it we may think of people who treat us badly or belittle or despise our opinions. To all of us Jesus says: 'Love them, do good to them, pray God's blessing on them. Dare to break the cycle of hatred, and you will be acting as children of God himself.'

That is what Jesus did himself. And where did it get him? To a cruel death on the cross, and his ideals destroyed with him. But the resurrection which followed his death shows that self-giving love always wins in the end.

Innocent man is crucified

This is a long passage, but the central event of the Christian story cannot be rushed.

Read Luke 23:1–56

The stirrings of opposition to Jesus have reached their climax. Jewish leaders have arrested him and have challenged him, 'Are you the Son of God?' But only

Pilate, the Roman governor, has authority to condemn a man to death. So to Pilate Jesus is taken.

His accusers try to get Pilate's support for the death sentence by claiming that Jesus is a serious threat to the country's political stability. Pilate is unimpressed by this and regards the case as just a tiresome dispute between religious groups. Herod Antipas, who by Rome's permission ruled over Galilee where Jesus was brought up, taunts Jesus but has no basis for condemning him.

Ironically, Jesus' accusers call for the release of a real terrorist, Barabbas, in order to secure the condemnation of a supposed terrorist, Jesus. And Pilate, to save his own skin, allows himself to be bullied into granting their demand.

So Jesus is led away to one of the most painful forms of execution ever devised. It was reserved by the Romans for slaves, foreigners and particularly violent criminals. He is mocked and humiliated to the end. But those who mock speak truth without knowing it. It is because Jesus refuses to save himself that he is able to save others. Through Jesus giving his life, God's love draws people to himself.

Even as Jesus dies he is calling down forgiveness on his executioners. And bringing hope to a criminal crucified alongside him.

Crucifixion: 'the most wretched of deaths'—Josephus, Jewish historian.

'... the very word "cross" should be far removed not only from the person of a Roman citizen but from his thoughts, his eyes and his ears'—Cicero, Roman statesman.

Witnesses confirm Jesus is raised from death!

Jesus' death was like thousands of other deaths in those times. But then something happened which marks him off as unique.

Read Luke 24:1–53

On the Sunday morning after Jesus' death, the shock-waves begin. Women find the tomb's entrance open, and the huge stone which sealed it rolled to one side. And the body of Jesus isn't there!

Has it been stolen? But who would have any reason to steal it? Bewildered, they suddenly see two angels gleaming with heavenly glory.

'Why do you look for the living among the dead?' they ask. 'He is not here. He has been raised to life!'

Even though Jesus has hinted that death would not be the end for him, the women find this too good to be true. And when Jesus' disciples hear their report, they mutter into their beards about hysterical women. The tomb may be empty, but *how*?

The stories of Cleopas and his friend, and of the risen Jesus later meeting his eleven disciples, show how the amazing truth dawned on them. The Jesus who had been dead and buried in the tomb is now alive!

He is not a man restored to earthly life, like someone who revives after lying in a coma. Nor is he a ghost. His earthly body has been raised and changed by God into a form fit for the everlasting life of heaven.

That is why his friends don't immediately recognize him. He isn't merely the same as he was before death. But then his words, his actions remind them of the Jesus they knew so well. So this Jesus, who has shown them more of God than they have ever glimpsed before, will stay with them for ever and share his life with theirs.

Jesus' followers went on to prove that this contact with Jesus was no one-off, peculiar experience. They began to tell the world how the man from Nazareth had opened the way to God. Despite tremendous opposition, they led many people to share their discovery that Jesus is alive and anyone can find him. But Luke needs another book to tell that story—the Acts of the Apostles.

The resurrection of Jesus is the *only* historically recorded event of its kind. It is God's way of saying to the first Christians and to us:

◆ **God's rescue of the human race from sin, a rescue which began way back in the history of the Jewish people, reached its climax in Jesus.**

Sin is the self-centred attitude that deliberately goes against what is right. It damages both ourselves and other people.

'Then they put him to death by nailing him to a cross. But God raised him from death three days later...'
Acts 10:39,40

'I am the resurrection and the life. He who believes in me will live, even though he dies...'
Jesus' words recorded in John 11:25

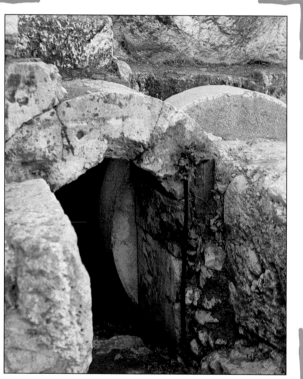

'But the truth is that Christ has been raised from death, as the guarantee that those who sleep in death will also be raised.'
1 Corinthians 15:20

◆ Jesus has opened the way for us through death into eternal life with God.

◆ God's power which raised Jesus from the grave is available to strengthen us when we live his way and share his love.

Amazing happenings—Jesus disappears!

About six weeks after Jesus rose from death, the appearances which he made to his followers came to an end. Luke's Gospel ends and the Acts of the Apostles begins with the story of Jesus' final appearance and return to God—the ascension.

He spoke to his friends about how they were to receive the power of God's Spirit to enable them to share with others the good news of his resurrection and his love for all people. And then 'he was taken up before their very eyes, and a cloud hid him from their sight'.

We may wonder exactly what kind of event these words are trying to describe. But probably Luke wants to tell us what the event *means* rather than what it looked like.

The ascension **marks the moment when Jesus' work on earth was complete** and he was welcomed to his Father's side as victor over death.

The ascension **prepared the way for the feast of Pentecost**, ten days later, when God would come to his people in a new way.

Because Jesus lived on earth as a human being, his work was restricted to particular times and places. But now that God expresses himself in the world in the form of the Holy Spirit, who filled the apostles at Pentecost, he is at work in all kinds of places and people at all times.

Jesus opened up the way to God for all people by showing us what God is like. His life and death and resurrection show a love so strong that it can even overcome death—a love that can cancel out our wrongdoings.

The ascension means that **Jesus has authority over his church and over his world**. Looking around at the world, we may wonder whether this is so. Evil and conflicts between human beings continue because Jesus does not force people to do his will.

Yet he has set limits to the power of evil. He is working towards his final victory, drawing people under the influence of his love. Christ's ascension points forward to the day when his defeat of evil, suffering and death will be complete and his people will be secure for ever in his presence.

4

Same story, different angle: the four Gospels

• • • • • • • • • • • • • •

You may wonder why four people bothered to write down the same story about the life of Jesus. Wouldn't one have been enough?

But when you want to find out the truth of a story, you go to the different people involved to get their angle on it.

Even eyewitness accounts of an event don't tally exactly—one person sees one detail clearly, someone else will bring out another point. And that's how it is with the four Gospels.

Luke is one of four people who wrote Gospels in the New Testament. Each Gospel-writer tells the story of Jesus in his own special way. Three of the Gospels— Matthew, Mark and Luke—contain material which is very similar. For instance, Jesus' teaching about what is demanded of those who follow him is found in Matthew 16:24–28, Mark 8:34–9:1 and Luke 9:23–27. It looks as though one writer has used another as a source for his own writing.

The Sermon on the Mount contains Jesus' famous teaching on how to be happy (or 'blessed') which turns normal expectations upside down. Mourners will be comforted, the meek will inherit the earth and those who are persecuted for doing right will inherit God's kingdom.

Blessed are the poor in spirit,
for theirs is the kingdom of heaven.

Blessed are those who mourn,
for they will be comforted.

Blessed are the meek,
for they will inherit the earth.

Blessed are those who hunger and thirst
for righteousness,
for they will be filled.

We can't be sure, but it seems most likely that Mark wrote his Gospel, the shortest one, first. Probably he was writing it for the church in Rome at a time of persecution, about AD 65—some thirty or so years after Jesus' death.

He gathered together stories which were familiar from the preaching and teaching of apostles such as Peter, and wrote them in a way which would encourage Christians in Rome as they faced the prospect of suffering for their faith. He emphasizes the sufferings of Jesus, as if to say, 'In your own suffering you are being faithful to your Lord and Master.'

Probably Matthew and Luke later copied parts of Mark and added other teachings of Jesus and stories about him which would particularly express what their readers needed to hear. Both of them included stories of Jesus' birth, which is not in Mark, and further stories about his resurrection.

Matthew added a lot of Jesus' teaching to what he found in Mark. The Sermon on the Mount, for example, gathers together key elements of Jesus' message about how to follow him. And Matthew was also concerned to show the relationship between Jesus and God's promises in the Old Testament made to the Jewish people.

Luke added incidents and teaching which illustrate Jesus' concern for the poor, the outcast and non-Jews. We see this, for example, in the reports of Jesus' first public teaching in the synagogue at his home town of Nazareth.

John's Gospel is rather different. It shows little sign of having been copied from the other three, and contains few of the stories found in them. Its style is more reflective, penetrating to the inner meaning of Jesus' life, death and resurrection.

Its famous beginning shows how the birth of Jesus was not a new thought on God's part, but was the result of God's eternal plan to communicate himself personally to men and women.

The Gospels give us four portraits of Jesus, each stressing some particular aspects of his life and his meaning for us, which together give us a full picture.

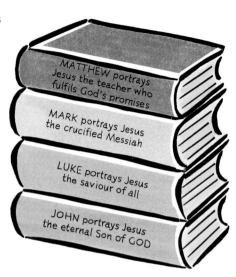

MATTHEW portrays Jesus the teacher who fulfils God's promises

MARK portrays Jesus the crucified Messiah

LUKE portrays Jesus the saviour of all

JOHN portrays Jesus the eternal Son of GOD

Jesus is called the Word of God because he is the ultimate way God has chosen to communicate with people—by becoming a human being.

In the beginning was the Word, and the Word was with God, and the Word was God . . . The Word became flesh and made his dwelling among us. We have seen his glory, the glory of the One and Only, who came from the Father, full of grace and truth.

JOHN 1:1, 14

5

Followers of Jesus: the Acts of the Apostles

● ● ● ● ● ● ● ● ● ● ● ● ● ●

If you think the church is dull, inward-looking and living in the past, you should look at the Acts of the Apostles! Here in his second volume Luke shows what the church of Jesus can be.

In the Acts of the Apostles ('Acts' for short) Luke selects events from the first thirty years of the church's life in order to show how the church continued the work which Jesus began. By the end of the book he has sketched the progress of the church's growth as far as Rome.

The first verse of Acts gives the reader a clue: 'In my former book, Theophilus, I wrote about all that Jesus *began* to do and to teach until the day he was taken up to heaven . . .' (italics mine).

What he has told us in his Gospel is only half the story. In his earthly life in Palestine Jesus made God real and conveyed his forgiveness, giving people new hope. But now he *continues* as the risen Lord to do the same for people in other places at other times.

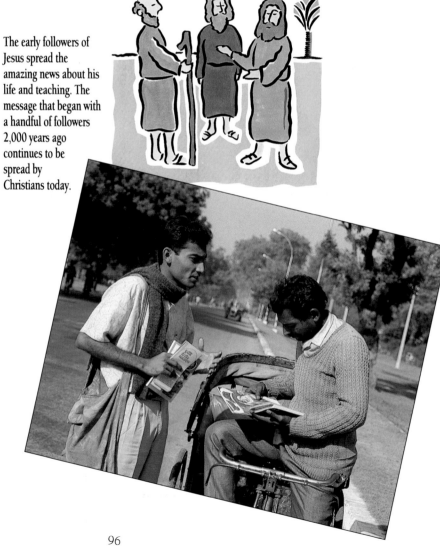

The early followers of Jesus spread the amazing news about his life and teaching. The message that began with a handful of followers 2,000 years ago continues to be spread by Christians today.

How to read the Acts of the Apostles

As with Luke's Gospel, there's a lot to be said for reading the book right through in one or two sittings. You get a sense of the overall shape of Acts if you notice how Luke divides the book up into six sections. Each section ends with a statement summing up 'the story so far', like the summaries in a magazine serial.

For example, the first summary says: 'So the word of God spread. The number of disciples in Jerusalem spread rapidly, and a large number of priests became obedient to the faith.'

This way of setting it out comes from the final words of the risen Jesus recorded in the first chapter of Acts: 'You will receive power when the Holy Spirit comes on you; and you will be my witnesses in Jerusalem, and in all Judea and Samaria, and to the ends of the earth.' Both that promise of Jesus and the shape of Luke's book suggest that his real concern is to tell people what the church is here for and how it has developed.

The book of Acts also introduces one of the great Christian leaders—Paul (whose Hebrew name was Saul), whose dramatic conversion to faith in Jesus Christ was a turning-point in the history of the church.

The six sections in Acts each describe one broad stage in the growth and expansion of the early church:

◆ **Acts 1:1–6:7**
   The earliest church in Jerusalem

◆ **Acts 6:8–9:31**
   The church grows into Samaria and beyond

◆ **Acts 9:32–12:24**
   The first outreach to Gentiles in Palestine and Syria

The news spreads

◆ Acts 12:25–16:5
Paul takes the good news to Cyprus and Asia
Minor (Turkey)

◆ Acts 16:6–19:20
Paul takes the good news into Europe

◆ Acts 19:21–28:31
Paul's mission finally takes him to Rome

The message of Acts

In telling how the church grew, Luke wants to emphasize certain aspects of the story.

Firstly, **the church gets its life from God's Holy Spirit**. The church is not simply a human organization, a club for people interested in religion. It exists because of what happened in Jerusalem at the festival of Pentecost, seven weeks after Jesus rose from the dead:

When the day of Pentecost came, they were all together in one place. Suddenly a sound like the blowing of

Love in action

Jackie Pullinger, who works among drug addicts in Hong Kong's notorious 'Walled City', tells how she learnt from experience that the church must reflect the mission of Jesus. Christians are to 'be' Jesus to people in need.

I tried to say 'Jesus loves you' in my best Cantonese, and they just said, 'What does that have to do with me?'

So I learnt that it was important not to say the word which nobody could understand. Why would anybody understand 'Jesus loves you' if they don't know who Jesus is and nobody has ever loved them? So I had to be Jesus to them rather than say the words. And that of course would mean things like—

if somebody has no money maybe giving them money,

if they had no food you'd give them yours,

or no house they could sleep in yours.

Or if they had no job it would mean finding them a job,
or visiting them in prison,
or walking an extra mile,
or giving your own clothes,
in fact sharing your life.
That's what I did, and over the years something went in . . .

Jackie Pullinger, in *The Law of Love*, Otter Productions

Many addicts have been set free from drugs by God's Spirit working through Jackie's team, and have found a new life in Jesus.

a violent wind came from heaven and filled the whole house where they were sitting. They saw what seemed to be tongues of fire that separated and came to rest on each of them. All of them were filled with the Holy Spirit and began to speak in other languages as the Spirit enabled them . . .

ACTS 2:1–4

This dramatic and mysterious account shows how Jesus' followers experienced God's power in a new way, as Jesus had promised them. The rest of chapter 2 shows how this event changed them.

It was the coming of God's Spirit—God's power—which enabled timid people to speak boldly about their faith in Jesus. It made them able to perform miracles of healing. It kept them faithful to Jesus when other people laughed at them or threatened their lives. It made them full of joy and generous concern for others.

And the rest of Acts shows how the church continued to develop because God's Spirit was at work in it.

Secondly, **the life and aims of the church mirror those of Jesus**. The earthly Jesus had a special concern for the poor, for outcasts, for people of different races and for all who were despised in Jewish society. And the church has the same concerns.

Thirdly, **people are brought to faith in Jesus through the preaching of God's message**. There is nothing Luke likes better than summarizing what Peter and Paul preached, and then telling us how those who heard them became followers of Christ.

So in the Acts of the Apostles Luke is telling the story of the early church's growth. By the way he presents the story, he wants to suggest what the church of Jesus should always be like. Christians should depend on God's power. They should reflect the concerns of Jesus. They should share the message of his love.

'You will be my witnesses... to the ends of the earth.' Jesus wants his church to show the same love to others as he did when he was on earth. This is the church's 'mission', to pass on the good news about Jesus.

Letter writing isn't as common today as it once was. In New Testament times it was an important method of long-distance communication. A large part of the New Testament contains letters written by an extraordinary man who became one of the early followers of Jesus. His name was Paul, and his advice to the new churches makes interesting reading.

6

'My love to all of you in Christ Jesus': Paul's letters

● ● ● ● ● ● ● ● ● ● ● ● ●

'I wish I could be with you during the present difficulties. For the moment that is impossible. But I haven't stopped thinking about you. And I am writing my advice in the hope that it may help you until I am able to be with you again . . .'

You may at some time have begun a letter rather like that. One of the reasons why we write letters is to say to our friends what we would say to them if we could be with them.

The first Christians wrote letters for the same reason. After nearly two thousand years, parts of the apostle Paul's letters are as real and as relevant as when they were first written—to Christians in Turkey, Greece and Rome. And these letters and others by Christian leaders are found after Acts in the New Testament.

The name 'Jesus Christ' was originally 'Jesus the Christ'—Jesus who is God's anointed one. 'Jesus' is in itself a significant name, meaning 'God saves'.

Paul was an amazing man by any yardstick. Brought up as a devout Jew, he became a teacher of the Jewish Law and persecuted the followers of Jesus until his dramatic meeting with the risen Christ on the road to Damascus. The story is told in Acts 9, and must have taken place between AD 32 and 35—that is, within about three years of Jesus' resurrection. From then on he became a fearless preacher of his new-found faith.

Many details of his missionary work are not recorded. The missionary journeys recorded in Acts 13–28 cover the period from about AD 46 to about AD 62. In those years of extensive travels, he covered at least 15,000 kilometres. Often he went hungry and thirsty. He faced dangers from bandits. He was imprisoned and flogged by people who hated his message or regarded him as a danger to the state. He was shipwrecked three or four times.

But he started up churches in many of the key cities of Turkey and Greece. As one of the great thinkers of the early church, he enabled new Christians to work out the meaning of Jesus' death and resurrection and to relate their faith to their everyday life. He showed how the life and message of a Palestinian preacher could leap over barriers of race and culture into the cosmopolitan world of Greece and Rome.

Paul wrote letters to Christians in churches throughout the Roman Empire. The New Testament preserves Paul's letters to the Romans, Corinthians, Galatians, Ephesians, Philippians, Colossians and Thessalonians, and to individual church leaders: Timothy, Titus and Philemon.

Paul's letters were mostly written to churches which he had founded, at places like Corinth, Thessalonica and Philippi. Two of them—the letters to Rome and Colossae—offered teaching and guidance to churches which other people had started. The short letters to Timothy, Titus and Philemon are addressed to individual church leaders.

Reading Paul's letters

When you start reading Paul's letters you realize that they are like other letters in several important ways. Most obviously, they are only one end of the correspondence, or conversation, between Paul and a particular church. You are reading someone else's mail, and some of it is explosive stuff!

Sometimes he makes clear that he is responding to an actual letter which the church has written to him (see 1 Corinthians). But we can only guess at what their letter said by reading between the lines of Paul's reply. This can be fun, though sometimes frustrating!

But we can be sure that he didn't write just to pass the time of day. Mostly he wrote to churches because they needed correcting in some way. This is not surprising, because they had all become Christians so recently.

Sometimes he wrote to a church which had misunderstood the essential gospel of Christ. For example, he wrote Galatians because people in the churches in the Roman province of Galatia (in Turkey) believed they could be followers of Jesus only by obeying the whole Jewish Law. On the contrary, Paul insisted, Jesus has won freedom for us by his death and resurrection. We become his people simply by receiving new life from him as a gift.

Sometimes Paul wrote to Christians who were in danger of confusing the truth about Christ with popular ideas from the surrounding world. The church at Colossae—the Colossians—got a letter from him showing how Christ reveals all that we need to know of God.

At other times he wrote to correct distorted ideas about Christian behaviour. The church at Corinth, for instance, was full of people who, in the name of 'Christian liberty', claimed that any kind of behaviour was acceptable to God. So in his second letter to the Corinthians Paul argued that our relationship with Jesus means that we should reflect his character in our lives.

His longest letter, Romans, was probably written partly to persuade Gentile Christians not to despise Jewish believers, whom they now outnumbered. It also gave him the opportunity to set out the message he

Jews expressed their relationship with God by keeping the Law. This included the Ten Commandments which God gave to Moses, as well as other regulations about circumcision and food preparation. Some Jewish Christians thought Gentile Christians could not be truly acceptable to God unless they observed all these regulations.

preached to a church which he had not yet visited. He hoped in this way to gain their support for a planned mission to Spain.

Other letters have more personal motives. In Philippians Paul thanks the Christians at Philippi for the love they have shown by sending him gifts, and he encourages them to stand firm in their faith. The little letter to a Christian called Philemon urges him to act leniently towards a runaway slave.

Whenever we read a New Testament letter we must do a little reading between the lines, asking *why* the situation may have made the writer want to stress these particular truths. This may sound difficult. But a bit of imagination, and discussion among friends, can make it very rewarding.

The important thing to remember is that the letters are not learned theories dreamt up in theologians' studies. They are responses to real people in real situations. They are forged in controversy, bursting with vitality. They are the outpourings of Paul's heart. And Paul was ready to give his life for the sake of the people who found new life through his preaching.

Paul's letters are not theories dreamed up by theologians—they are addressed to real people in real situations.

Every letter is written out of the concern for people with which Paul signs off his letter to Corinth: 'My love to all of you in Christ Jesus.'

Reading the New Testament letters today

Even though the New Testament letters are nearly two thousand years old, some parts of them are easy to understand and to relate to our own lives. For instance, when we read the famous passage about love in 1 Corinthians 13, our difficulty is not in understanding what it means. The main problem lies in living up to its demand.

But other parts of the letters cannot be related so

Bothersome reading

Most people are bothered by those passages in Scripture which they cannot understand; but as for me, I always noticed that the passages in Scripture which troubled me most are those I do understand.

Mark Twain

---

readily to our own lives. We now live in very different circumstances. Some letters, for example, give guidance about how Christian slaves and slave-owners ought to behave. Such teaching was necessary in a society where slavery was normal and was not going to be abolished in a hurry.

But what do these instructions mean in societies which have at last learnt from the Christian message that slavery degrades humanity? We can't apply them automatically to the modern work-situation in a factory or on a farm because workers aren't slaves. They aren't owned by their employers.

What we can do is to draw *principles* from such teaching which will help our thinking about work and relationships between employer and employee. Ephesians may suggest four principles:

◆ **A trustworthy attitude to work is part of our Christian responsibility. We show our commitment to Christ in the workplace as much as anywhere else.**

◆ **Work is transformed when we recognize that ultimately our responsibility is to Christ rather than to an earthly master. This doesn't mean that repetitive, boring work suddenly becomes exciting. But it can mean that the whole work scene is changed when we relate to our colleagues and employers in the same way as we try to relate to Christ.**

◆ All of us—whether slave or master, employee or employer—must give account of our lives to God. Therefore we must aim to work in a way which will please him.

◆ Employers should recognize that their earthly status brings them no special privileges with God. Power carries responsibility. Because they have power to change things, they have a special duty to create a work environment which embodies the belief that people matter more than profit.

Once we have seen what basic principles may be suggested by the New Testament, we can go on to use our God-given minds to work out how the principles might be applied in a particular situation. The New Testament is not like a map giving detailed instructions for every situation we might meet. It is like a compass to point us in the right direction.

Getting started on Paul's letters

Paul's most famous letters are probably Romans and 1 Corinthians. But both letters are quite long. So if you've never read a New Testament letter carefully before, it is a good idea to read a short, more straightforward one first.

Paul's short letter to the Philippians, for example, shows him writing to a church with which he has had a warm relationship for several years. He writes from prison, probably in Rome about AD62, to thank them for a gift of money which has brought great encouragement. In the course of the letter we can learn about prayer, about how God can bring good out of our sufferings, about who Jesus is, about true Christian living, and much else besides.

Other Christian leaders apart from Paul wrote letters which can be found in the New Testament—the letter to

Outline of Philippians

1:1–11   Greetings, thanksgiving and prayer
1:12–26   Paul's imprisonment can't stop the good news
           being heard
1:27–2:18 A plea for unity and Christ-like humility
2:19–30   Paul commends his fellow-workers, Timothy
           and Epaphroditus
3:1–4:1   A warning about false teachers
4:2–9   Paul encourages the Philippians
4:10–20   Thanks for the gift sent by the Philippians
4:21–23   Final greetings

the Hebrews, and letters from James, Peter and John. The variety of issues with which they deal gives some idea of the variety of the first-century churches. Even within fifty years of Jesus' resurrection, church communities were spread far and wide, facing challenges to their beliefs and their lifestyle from many different directions.

The varied nature of these documents helps to ensure that, whatever challenges confront us today, there is a word from the New Testament to guide us.

Whatever challenges us today, the New Testament can show us God's perspective on our situation.

7

Too hot to handle?: the book of Revelation

● ● ● ● ● ● ● ● ● ● ● ● ●

The New Testament's most difficult book comes last, and the difficulty of understanding it has led many Christians to leave it well alone.

Others, making the most of its strange picture-language, have claimed to find in it detailed schemes of the progress of world history towards its end.

But the book of Revelation is not quite so difficult if we take seriously its own clues about its purpose and meaning.

From the opening chapter we notice three things about it:

Firstly, it is a 'revelation from Jesus Christ' about 'what must soon take place'. That word 'revelation' translates the Greek *apokalypsis*, from which we get our words 'apocalypse' and 'apocalyptic'. By giving it this title the author is telling us that his book belongs to the kind of writing known as 'apocalyptic literature'.

There were many examples of Jewish apocalyptic literature. Parts of some Old Testament books—Ezekiel and Daniel, for example—and some New Testament passages, such as Mark 13, have a similar style. It was written when times were bad. People who had experienced intense suffering at the hands of hostile rulers pinned their hope on God creating a new world of justice and peace.

Such literature often gives 'timetables' of God's plans in history which look as though precise predictions are being offered. But the real purpose of these 'predictions' is to suggest that God's purpose *will* triumph in the end,

---

Outline of Revelation

1:1–20	Prologue: greetings, and John's vision of Christ
2:1–3:22	Messages to the seven churches of Asia
4:1–5:14	A glimpse into heaven, where it is revealed that the saving work of Christ is the key to understanding God's purpose in history
6:1–17, 8:1	The seven seals: a symbolic description of events leading up to the final coming of Christ
7:1–17	First interlude: the church is secure in God's care
8:2—9:21, 11:15–19	The seven trumpets: a further symbolic description of events leading up to the final coming of Christ
10:1–11:14	Second interlude: the church's task, to witness in the face of suffering
12:1–14:20	Third interlude: conflict between the church and evil powers
15:1–16:21	The seven bowls of God's wrath: a further symbolic description of events leading up to the final coming of Christ
17:1–19:10	The fall of 'Babylon': Rome's anti-Christian empire falls prey to its own forces of destruction
19:11–21	Christ's final coming
20:1–10	The reign of Christ and the destruction of Satan
20:11–15	The final judgment
21:1–22:5	The new heaven and the new earth
22:6–21	Epilogue: concluding promises and warnings

not to tell us exactly *when* it will happen.

Apocalypses also enjoy using picture-language which is strange to us—beasts, dragons, plagues, for example. These symbols would be no more strange to the readers of Revelation than football and Coca-Cola are to us.

It may involve us in some effort to find out what the symbols mean. But if we look at other writings from the New Testament period the meanings are there to be discovered. The fault in many modern interpretations of Revelation is that they *impose* a meaning on the picture-language of the book without troubling to ask what it would have meant to the book's first readers, in the context of first-century Christianity.

Secondly, this book is also prophecy. Like Old Testament prophets, the author of this book speaks God's word to particular situations. He expresses God's warnings of judgment and promises of deliverance. We can see this most clearly in chapters 2 and 3, which contain messages to seven churches. These messages look very like some Old Testament prophetic statements, with their warnings and encouragements.

Thirdly, Revelation is also a letter. The author uses the same kind of opening greeting which can be found in other New Testament letters (see Philippians). He identifies himself as John. It is often assumed that this is the apostle John, one of Jesus' original twelve followers. But he doesn't call himself an apostle, and may be someone else of the same name.

His readers are 'the seven churches in the province of Asia', in what we now call Western Turkey. Like any letter writer, John expects his letter to be understood by its first readers. And he has their particular circumstances in mind. He is not writing coded messages for future generations, but challenging his readers and warning them in the light of persecution which he sees coming their way.

Many of the early Christians were sentenced to death by the Roman authorities for following Jesus. In parts of the world today, Christians are persecuted because of their faith. The last book of the Bible contains a powerful message of hope for all who are oppressed or in danger.

Revelation for today

When Christians in stable and tolerant democracies neglect the book of Revelation, they are showing a lack of sympathy for their brothers and sisters who face persecution for their faith. This book has always 'come alive' for Christians who find themselves in danger similar to the oppression by the Roman authorities which threatened John's first readers.

John was probably writing during the reign of the emperor Domitian (AD 81–96). When Domitian issued a decree demanding to be called 'Lord and God', Christians' loyalty to Christ as the one Lord made them unable to submit to this absolute demand.

As persecution threatened, they would be asking, 'Where is God in all this? Does power really lie in God's hands, or in Domitian's?' John responds by showing them a Christ who was himself 'the faithful witness' in the face of suffering and is now 'the ruler of the kings of the earth'.

To Christians fearful for the future this Christ declares, 'Do not be afraid. I am the First and the Last. I am the Living One; I was dead, and behold I am alive for ever and ever!'

Christ has gone through suffering before us, and goes through suffering with us now.

John points his readers to the Christ who has gone through suffering before them, and goes through their sufferings with them now. His victory over death is the guarantee that in the end God's purpose will triumph. Christ will come again one day to bring the course of history to its end. He will welcome his people into the 'new heaven and new earth' which is his destiny for them.

In encouraging his readers to face suffering, John is writing out of his own experience. He himself has suffered exile to the island of Patmos because of his Christian witness. And what he writes is not the ramblings of his mind, but a vision given to him by the risen Christ.

We may never understand all the details. But there remains much that we can gain from it, if we keep asking it the right questions:

◆ **What comfort does it offer to Christians threatened by persecution?**

◆ **What challenge does it offer Christians to maintain a distinctive lifestyle despite the pressures to conform to the surrounding society?**

◆ **What warnings does it give to a godless world?**

◆ **What does it say about the task of the church in the face of conflict?**

◆ **How does our ultimate hope of eternal life influence our attitude to life now?**

8

A message for today

●●●●●●●●●●●●●

We have explored how the New Testament books came to be written. We have thought about the message they contain. But the question remains: why should such old books influence people's lives today?

Why should we take notice of them? How can they guide our lives when our world is so different from the world of the first Christians?

Certainly most people's experience of the world is very different from that of first-century people. The development of science and medicine, travel and education has raised for us questions of which the first Christians knew nothing.

We face moral questions about abortion and about Aids. We have the ability to devastate the world in an instant through nuclear weapons, or more slowly through pollution of the environment. We are in desperate need of guidance in such matters. But the Bible says nothing directly about them.

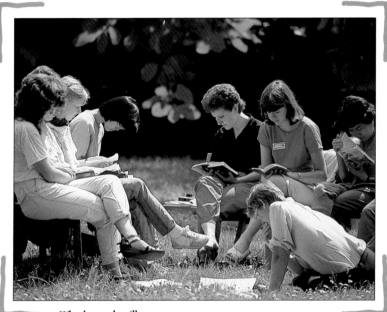

Why do people still
read the New
Testament now?
Because it answers the
questions and
addresses the needs of
people of every age
and culture.

The Bible speaks today

Yet Christians still find no book is so life-giving, so indispensable as the Bible. Why is this? There are several reasons why it continues to speak across the centuries.

Though the world has changed in many ways, some things have changed very little since New Testament times. Human nature does not change. We are still the same bundles of hopes and fears, of guilt and generosity, of self-seeking and self-giving, as the people whom Jesus and Luke and Paul met. We have the same basic needs and the same questions about life as they did.

We need a purpose for life that is more than material comfort. We wonder what lies beyond death. Millions are gripped by the fear of fate and the power of astrology, just as the Greek readers of Paul's letters were. We wonder how people of different races and social classes can live in harmony, and we can find new hope just as first-century Christians did when they saw God breaking down barriers between Jews and Gentiles, rich and poor, slaves and free people. We know the power of evil and the need of forgiveness.

So it is no surprise that people in many cultures speak of the Bible not only as a book which they read, but as the book which reads them.

In actual experience people all over the world constantly find that the New Testament speaks to them in a vital, up-to-date way. When you think about it, it's quite extraordinary how this small book, written in the cultures of ancient Palestine, Greece and Rome, should communicate today to people in every culture under the sun.

The Bible is able to speak to people in all the varied situations of life because, as Christians believe, it is 'inspired' by God. Although it is a human book, produced through the normal processes of writing, it is also a divine book.

When Luke wrote his Gospel, as we have seen, he did research to establish the facts as any other historian might have done. When Paul wrote his letters, he responded to questions raised by his churches as any other concerned pastor might have done. That is the human aspect of their writing.

But because Luke was recording the life and words of Jesus, and because Paul was called personally to be Christ's apostle, there is a special sense in which they are giving us God's word. That is the divine aspect of their writing.

Paul's second letter to Timothy makes this claim:

All Scripture is God-breathed and is useful for teaching, rebuking, correcting and training in righteousness, so that the man of God may be thoroughly equipped for every good work.

2 TIMOTHY 3:16

A changed heart

A village tyrant in Sri Lanka ruled his neighbourhood with an iron fist. Amaradasa had become rich from illegal brewing and killing cattle for beef. One woman after another was bullied into sharing his home. The whole village lived in fear of him.

His friend had been given a booklet which presented the Bible's teaching on various themes. As he read what it said about forgiveness he found new hope for himself and thought, 'This is certainly good news for me. But even more for my friend.'

The man gave the booklet to Amaradasa, who read and re-read it. At first he was tense, bitter. Then slowly he relaxed and began to smile. From that moment his friend noticed a change, which could only be the work of God in his life.

At first Amaradasa wanted to honour the miraculous message, so he fixed the paper on the wall of his house and began to worship it. But he found no peace in his heart. Finally, he wrote to the Bible Society which had produced the booklet, asking for help. Six months later, he was at the centre of a young and growing church, serving the village he had terrorized.

He is referring to the Old Testament here, since at the time of writing the New Testament had not been brought together as a collection of books. But it is reasonable to think that the God who inspired the Old Testament would also give us documents which show the fulfilment of its promises in the coming of Jesus.

The books of the New Testament, written as they were by the apostles or by people who were very close to them, are the earliest witness to Jesus that exists. They are the closest we can get to his life and to the first impact of his death and resurrection. No other Christian documents are so early or so full of first-hand testimony.

It is impossible to *prove* that the Bible is specially inspired by God. It is a matter of faith—and of personal experience. For down through the centuries Christians have found that through its pages they meet with God and come into an experience of his love. By it they are challenged, guided and kept in Christ's way.

9

A message for me

●●●●●●●●●●●●●●

Understanding the message of the New Testament is one thing. Acting on it is another.

Big claims are made for its influence on people now, though it describes events of two thousand years ago. But how exactly does it speak to our lives? And what should our response be?

We might think of the New Testament as speaking to us in three ways:

Firstly, it speaks about **our relationship with God**. For instance, the teaching of Jesus in the Gospels and parts of the New Testament letters tell us what God is like. Stories in the Gospels about people meeting Jesus show how we can come to him to find forgiveness, healing and new life. Teaching in the letters shows how our relationship with him can grow through our experience of God's Spirit in us and our obedience to his guidance.

Secondly, it speaks about **our relationship to God's people, the church**. The books of the Bible were written mainly for a community, not for individuals. It's important—especially for people who do not enjoy reading on their own—to realize that the natural context for learning what the Bible says and means is a group of Christians. This might be a large group listening together to a sermon which explains a Bible passage. Or a small group of people discussing it, arguing about it, struggling to work out its meaning for their lives together.

This is how most Christians grow towards maturity in their faith. This is how God shows the world that he is real and active—as a group of Christians learn from the New Testament how to live in Christ-like love towards each other and towards the rest of society.

Thirdly, it speaks about **our relationship to society and to the world**. It shows us a God who cares about the world he has made, who longs that men and women should come to know his love and should care for each other. And it shows how Christians are meant to reflect in their own lives God's character and his concern for the world. It is full of examples of what it means in particular circumstances to 'love the Lord your God ... and your neighbour as yourself'.

The New Testament will not give us ready-made answers about how to respond to dilemmas in the modern world which were unknown to the biblical writers. It isn't a cook-book with a detailed recipe for every modern situation. It doesn't treat us as children needing to be told exactly what to do all the time.

Instead, the Bible's message gradually makes us the people we are meant to be—people of love and insight, able to think wisely and responsibly about God's will for the present. **The Bible makes the Christian, and the Christian responds to situations in a Christ-like way.**

Taking the Bible's message seriously gradually changes Christians into the people God made them to be.

Having the right approach

If we are to come close to God and to benefit from reading the Bible, it's important to approach it with a

The New Testament clearly shows that caring for one another and putting the needs of others before our own are essential parts of the Christian life.

healthy attitude. I suggest the following guidelines:

◆ Have an attitude of listening to God. Expect him to speak to you—to teach, challenge and encourage you through the words of the Bible.

◆ Pray for the Holy Spirit's guidance. Because the Bible was inspired by God, God's Spirit will help us to understand and apply it to our lives.

◆ Expect to learn from the experiences of other Christians as you study the Bible with them. Because of who they are and what they've been through, they will notice things in a passage which haven't occurred to you. And you will have insights to share with them.

◆ Ask God to show you what action your study should lead to. Then he will gradually change you, and will change the world through you and others like you. But Bible study is of no value unless it leads to action. Jesus said:

I will show you what he is like who comes to me and hears my words and puts them into practice. He is like a man building a house, who dug deep down and laid the foundation on rock. When the flood came, the torrent struck that house but could not shake it, because it was well built. But the one who hears my words and does not put them into practice is like a man who built a house on the ground without a foundation. The moment the torrent struck that house, it collapsed and its destruction was complete.

LUKE 6:47–49

Ask and it will be given to you;
seek and you will find; knock
and the door will be opened to you.
For everyone who asks receives;
he who seeks finds; and to him who
knocks, the door will be opened.

JESUS' WORDS RECORDED IN MATTHEW 7:7–8

Come near to God and he will come
near to you.

JAMES 4:8

Whoever comes to me I will never
drive away.

JESUS' WORDS RECORDED IN JOHN 6:37

Text acknowledgments
All Scripture quotations in this publication are from
the HOLY BIBLE, NEW INTERNATIONAL VERSION.
Copyright © 1973, 1978, 1984 by the International Bible
Society. Used by permission.

Picture acknowledgments
Part 1: Starting with the Old Testament
Illustrations and maps by Tony de Saulles
Photographs by Lion Publishing 41 (David Alexander),
7 (David Townsend); 18, 29, 56 (British Museum);
31 (Hutchison Library); 9 (all) (Skjold Photography);
16, 63 (ZEFA).
Part 2: Starting with the New Testament
Illustrations and maps by Tony de Saulles
Photographs by Ebenezer Pictures, 117 (Susanna Burton),
96 (James Heard), 123 (C and J Pemberton); Lion Publishing,
79 (David Alexander), 88 (David Townsend); 113 (Telegraph
Colour Library); 68 (ZEFA).